LIGUORI CATHOLIC BIBLE STUDY

Historical Books I

JOSHUA, JUDGES, RUTH, 1 AND 2 SAMUEL

WILLIAM A. ANDERSON, DMIN, PHD

Liguori
LIGUORI, MISSOURI

Imprimi Potest:
Harry Grile, CSsR, Provincial
Denver Province, The Redemptorists

Printed with Ecclesiastical Permission and Approved for Private or Instructional Use

Nihil Obstat: Rev. Msgr. Kevin Michael Quirk, JCD, JV
               Censor Librorum

Imprimatur: + Michael J. Bransfield
               Bishop of Wheeling-Charleston [West Virginia]
               April 22, 2013

Published by Liguori Publications
Liguori, Missouri 63057

To order, call 800-325-9521
www.liguori.org

Copyright © 2013 William A. Anderson

Library of Congress Cataloging-in-Publication Data

Anderson, William Angor, 1937-
    Historical books I : Joshua, Judges, Ruth, 1 and 2 Samuel / William A. Anderson, DMin, PhD.—
First Edition. pages cm
1. Bible. O.T. Joshua—Commentaries. 2. Bible. O.T. Judges—Commentaries. 3. Bible. O.T. Ruth—Commentaries. 4. Bible. O.T. Samuel—Commentaries. I. Title.
    BS1295.53.A53 2013
    222'.07—dc23

                                              2013006374

p ISBN: 978-0-7648-2133-2
e ISBN: 978-0-7648-6839-9

Liguori Publications, a nonprofit corporation, is an apostolate of the Redemptorists. To learn more about the Redemptorists, visit Redemptorists.com.

Printed in the United States of America
17 16 15 14 13 / 5 4 3 2 1
First Edition

Contents

> NOTE: The length of each Bible section varies. Group leaders should combine sections as needed to fit the number of sessions in their program.

Acknowledgments

Bible studies and reflections depend on the help of others who read the manuscript and make suggestions. I am especially indebted to Sister Anne Francis Bartus, CSJ, DMin, whose vast experience and knowledge were very helpful in bringing this series to its final form.

This series is lovingly dedicated to the memory of my parents, Kathleen and Angor Anderson, in gratitude for all they shared with all who knew them, especially my siblings and me.

About the Author

William A. Anderson, DMin, PhD, is a presbyter of the diocese of Wheeling-Charleston, West Virginia. A director of retreats and parish missions, professor, catechist, spiritual director, and a former pastor, he has written extensively on pastoral, spiritual, and religious subjects. Father Anderson earned his doctor of ministry degree from St. Mary's Seminary & University in Baltimore and his doctorate in sacred theology from Duquesne University in Pittsburgh.

Introduction to
Liguori Catholic Bible Study

READING THE BIBLE can be daunting. It's a complex book, and many a person of goodwill has tried to read the Bible and ended up putting it down in utter confusion. It helps to have a companion, and _Liguori Catholic Bible Study_ is a solid one. Over the course of this series, you'll learn about biblical messages, themes, personalities, and events and understand how the books of the Bible rose out of the need to address new situations.

Across the centuries, people of faith have asked, "Where is God in this moment?" Millions of Catholics look to the Bible for encouragement in their journey of faith. Wisdom teaches us not to undertake Bible study alone, disconnected from the Church that was given Scripture to share and treasure. When used as a source of prayer and thoughtful reflection, the Bible comes alive.

Your choice of a Bible-study program should be dictated by what you want to get out of it. One goal of _Liguori Catholic Bible Study_ is to give readers greater familiarity with the Bible's structure, themes, personalities, and message. But that's not enough. This program will also teach you to use Scripture in your prayer. God's message is as compelling and urgent today as ever, but we get only part of the message when it's memorized and stuck in our heads. It's meant for the entire person—physical, emotional, and spiritual.

We're baptized into life with Christ, and we're called to live more fully with Christ today as we practice the values of justice, peace, forgiveness, and community. God's new covenant was written on the hearts of the people of Israel; we, their spiritual descendants, are loved that intimately by God today. _Liguori Catholic Bible Study_ will draw you closer to God, in whose image and likeness we are fashioned.

Group and Individual Study

The *Liguori Catholic Bible Study* series is intended for group and individual study and prayer. This series gives you the tools to start a study group. Gathering two or three people in a home or announcing the meeting of a Bible-study group in a parish or community can bring surprising results. Each lesson in this series contains a section to help groups study, reflect, pray, and share biblical reflections. Each lesson, except the first, also has a second section for individual study.

Many people who want to learn more about the Bible don't know where to begin. This series gives them a place to start and helps them continue until they're familiar with all the books of the Bible.

Bible study can be a lifelong project, always enriching those who wish to be faithful to God's Word. When people complete a study of the whole Bible, they can begin again, making new discoveries with each new adventure into the Word of God.

Lectio Divina (Sacred Reading)

BIBLE STUDY isn't just a matter of gaining intellectual knowledge of the Bible; it's also about gaining a greater understanding of God's love and concern for creation. The purpose of reading and knowing the Bible is to enrich our relationship with God. God loves us and gave us the Bible to illustrate that love. As Emeritus Pope Benedict XVI reminds us, a study of the Bible is not only an intellectual pursuit but also a spiritual adventure that should influence our dealings with God and neighbor.

The Meaning of *Lectio Divina*

Lectio divina is a Latin expression that means "divine or sacred reading." The process for *lectio divina* consists of Scripture readings, reflection, and prayer. Many clergy, religious, and laity use *lectio divina* in their daily spiritual reading to develop a closer and more loving relationship with God. Learning about Scripture has as its purpose the living of its message, which demands a period of reflection on the Scripture passages.

Prayer and *Lectio Divina*

Prayer is a necessary element for the practice of *lectio divina*. The entire process of reading and reflecting is a prayer. It's not merely an intellectual pursuit; it's also a spiritual one. Page 16 includes an Opening Prayer for gathering one's thoughts before moving on to the passages in each section. This prayer may be used privately or in a group. For those who use the book for daily spiritual reading, the prayer for each section may be repeated each day. Some may wish to keep a journal of each day's meditation.

Pondering the Word of God

Lectio divina is the ancient Christian spiritual practice of reading the holy Scriptures with intentionality and devotion. This practice helps Christians center themselves and descend to the level of the heart to enter an inner quiet space, finding God.

This sacred reading is distinct from reading for knowledge or information, and it's more than the pious practice of spiritual reading. It is the practice of opening ourselves to the action and inspiration of the Holy Spirit. As we intentionally focus on and become present to the inner meaning of the Scripture passage, the Holy Spirit enlightens our minds and hearts. We come to the text willing to be influenced by a deeper meaning that lies within the words and thoughts we ponder.

In this space, we open ourselves to be challenged and changed by the inner meaning we experience. We approach the text in a spirit of faith and obedience as a disciple ready to be taught by the Holy Spirit. As we savor the sacred text, we let go of our usual control of how we expect God to act in our lives and surrender our hearts and consciences to the flow of the divine (*divina*) through the reading (*lectio*).

The fundamental principle of *lectio divina* leads us to understand the profound mystery of the Incarnation, "The Word became flesh," not only in history but also within us.

Praying *Lectio* Today

Before you begin, relax your body and maintain a posture of prayer (back straight, eyes shut, feet flat on the floor). Then practice these four simple actions:

1. Read a passage from Scripture or the daily Mass readings. This is known as *lectio*. (If the Word of God is read aloud, the hearers listen attentively.)

2. Pray the selected passage with attention as you listen for a specific meaning that comes to mind. Once again, the reading is listened to or silently read and reflected or meditated on. This is known as *meditatio*.

3. The exercise becomes active. Pick a word, sentence, or idea that surfaces from your consideration of the chosen text. Does the reading remind you of a person, place, or experience? If so, pray about it. Compose your thoughts and reflection into a simple word or phrase. This prayer-thought will help you remove distractions during the *lectio*. This exercise is called *oratio*.

4. In silence, with your eyes closed, quiet yourself and become conscious of your breathing. Let your thoughts, feelings, and concerns fade as you consider the selected passage in the previous step (*oratio*). If you're distracted, use your prayer word to help you return to silence. This is *contemplatio*.

This exercise can take as long as you want, but in the context of this Bible study, 10 to 20 minutes should be sufficient.

Many teachers of prayer call contemplation the prayer of resting in God, a prelude to losing oneself in the presence of God. Scripture is transformed in our hearing as we pray and allow our hearts to unite intimately with the Lord. The Word truly takes on flesh, and this time it is manifested in our flesh.

How to Use This Bible-Study Companion

THE BIBLE, along with the commentaries and reflections found in this study, will help participants become familiar with the Scripture texts and lead them to reflect more deeply on the texts' message. At the end of this study, participants will have a firm grasp of Joshua, Judges, Ruth, First Samuel, and Second Samuel, becoming therefore more cognizant of the spiritual nourishment these books offer. This study is not only an intellectual adventure, it's also a spiritual one. The reflections lead participants into their own journey with the Scripture readings.

Context

When the authors wrote the historical books, they didn't simply link random stories together. Rather, they placed them in a context to stress a message. To help readers learn about each passage in relation to those around it, each lesson begins with an overview that puts the Scripture passages into context.

Part 1: Group Study

To give participants a comprehensive study of these historical books, the book is divided into eight lessons. Lesson 1 is group study only; Lessons 2 through 8 are divided into Part 1, group study, and Part 2, individual study. For example, Lesson 2 covers passages from Joshua 5 through 24. The study group reads and discusses only Joshua 5—7 (Part 1). Participants privately read and reflect on Joshua 8 through 24 (Part 2).

Group study may or may not include *lectio divina*. With *lectio divina,* the group meets for ninety minutes using the format at the top of page 14. Without *lectio divina*, the group meets for one hour using the format at the bottom of page 14, and participants are urged to privately read the *lectio divina* section at the end of Part 1. It contains additional reflections on the Scripture passages studied during the group session that will take participants even further into the passages.

Part 2: Individual Study

The Scripture passages not covered in Part 1 are divided into shorter components, one to be studied each day. Participants who don't belong to a study group can use the lessons for private sacred reading. They may choose to reflect on one Scripture passage per day, making it possible for a clearer understanding of the Scripture passages used in their *lectio divina* (sacred reading).

A PROCESS FOR SACRED READING

Liguori Publications has designed this study to be user friendly and manageable. However, group dynamics and leaders vary. We're not trying to keep the Holy Spirit from working in your midst, thus we suggest you decide beforehand which format works best for your group. If you have limited time, you could study the Bible as a group and save prayer and reflection for personal time.

However, if your group wishes to digest and feast on sacred Scripture through both prayer and study, we recommend you spend closer to ninety minutes each week by gathering to study and pray with Scripture. *Lectio divina* (see page 9) is an ancient contemplative prayer form that moves readers from the head to the heart in meeting the Lord. We strongly suggest using this prayer form whether in individual or group study.

GROUP-STUDY FORMATS

1. Bible Study With *Lectio Divina*

About ninety minutes of group study

- ✠ Gathering and opening prayer (3–5 minutes)
- ✠ Scripture passage read aloud (5 minutes)
- ✠ Silently review the commentary and prepare to discuss it with the group (3–5 minutes)
- ✠ Discuss the Scripture passage along with the commentary and reflection (30 minutes)
- ✠ Scripture passage read aloud a second time, followed by quiet time for meditation and contemplation (5 minutes)
- ✠ Spend some time in prayer with the selected passage. Group participants will slowly read the Scripture passage a third time in silence, listening for the voice of God as they read (10–20 minutes)
- ✠ Shared reflection (10–15 minutes)
- ✠ Closing prayer (3–5 minutes)

To become acquainted with lectio divina, *see page 9.*

2. Bible Study

About one hour of group study

- ✠ Gathering and opening prayer (3–5 minutes)
- ✠ Scripture passage read aloud (5 minutes)
- ✠ Silently review the commentary and prepare to discuss it with the group (3–5 minutes)
- ✠ Discuss the Scripture passage along with the commentary and reflection (40 minutes)
- ✠ Closing prayer (3–5 minutes)

Notes to the Leader

- ☩ Bring a copy of the *New American Bible,* revised edition.
- ☩ Plan which sections will be covered each week of your Bible study.
- ☩ Read the material in advance of each session.
- ☩ Establish written ground rules. (Example: We won't keep you longer than ninety minutes; don't dominate the sharing by arguing or debating.)
- ☩ Meet in an appropriate and welcoming gathering space (church building, meeting room, house).
- ☩ Provide name tags and perhaps use a brief icebreaker for the first meeting; ask participants to introduce themselves.
- ☩ Mark the Scripture passage(s) that will be read during the session.
- ☩ Decide how you would like the Scripture to be read aloud (whether by one or multiple readers).
- ☩ Use a clock or watch.
- ☩ Provide extra Bibles (or copies of the Scripture passages) for participants who don't bring their Bible.
- ☩ Ask participants to read "Introduction: Historical Books I" (page 17) before the first session.
- ☩ Tell participants which passages to study and urge them to read the passages and commentaries before the meeting.
- ☩ If you opt to use the *lectio divina* format, familiarize yourself with this prayer form ahead of time.

Notes to Participants

- ☩ Bring a copy of the *New American Bible,* revised edition.
- ☩ Read "Introduction: Historical Books I" (page 17) before the first session.
- ☩ Read the Scripture passages and commentaries before each session.
- ☩ Be prepared to share and listen respectfully. (This is not a time to debate beliefs or argue.)

Opening Prayer

Leader: O God, come to my assistance.

Response: O Lord, make haste to help me.

Leader: Glory be to the Father, and to the Son, and to the Holy Spirit...

Response: ...as it was in the beginning, is now, and ever shall be, world without end. Amen.

Leader: Christ is the vine and we are the branches. As branches linked to Jesus, the vine, we are called to recognize that the Scriptures are always being fulfilled in our lives. It is the living Word of God living on in us. Come, Holy Spirit, fill the hearts of your faithful and kindle in us the fire of your divine wisdom, knowledge, and love.

Response: Open our minds and hearts as we study your great love for us as shown in the Bible.

Reader: (Open your Bible to the assigned Scripture(s) and read in a paced, deliberate manner. Pause for one minute, listening for a word, phrase, or image that you may use in your *lectio divina* practice.)

Closing Prayer

Leader: Let us pray as Jesus taught us.

Response: Our Father...

Leader: Lord, inspire us with your Spirit as we study your Word in the Bible. Be with us this day and every day as we strive to know you and serve you and to love as you love. We believe that through your goodness and love, the Spirit of the Lord is truly upon us. Allow the words of the Bible, your Word, to capture us and inspire us to live as you live and to love as you love.

Response: Amen.

Leader: May the divine assistance remain with us always.

Response: In the name of the Father, and of the Son, and of the Holy Spirit. Amen.

Historical Books I

Read this overview before the first session.

A pastor, who used stories in his homilies, jokingly said in one of his Sunday homilies, "All my stories are true, and some of them really happened!" He never worried about the truthfulness of the stories he used as long as they seemed plausible and enabled his audience to connect their life stories to his story. He sometimes embellished and idealized some of his stories as long as he believed the story had a lesson to teach. The pastor said his stories were true because they touched upon many of the true emotions and struggles of a person's life.

In reading the historical books of the Bible, the reader is on an imaginative journey of stories that happened in essence but which were embellished and idealized as they passed by word-of-mouth from one generation to the next before they were finally written down. The historical books belong to the Bible, the inspired Word of God. It is the message that is important, not the exact history. The historical books of the Bible tell us that God was at work in the history of Israel. In these books, there are some historical facts, some embellishments and exaggerations, idealized stories of characters portrayed, biased presentations, and deep faith in God as the one true God.

Sagas in the Early Israelite Community

After reading the first five books of the Bible (Pentateuch), the reader encounters the historical books, which contain the Books of Joshua, Judges, First and Second Samuel, First and Second Kings, First and Second Chronicles, Ezra, and Nehemiah. Although the Book of Ruth does not strictly belong to the historical books, it is placed before First Samuel in our current Bible since it includes the story of the grandmother of David. In this volume of *Liguori Catholic Bible Study*, we will study the Books of Joshua, Judges, Ruth, First Samuel, and Second Samuel. The remaining historical books (First and Second Kings, First and Second Chronicles, Ezra, and Nehemiah) will be studied in a later volume.

In the historical books, the reader meets some of the major heroes and villains of Old Testament history. Scholars concede that the contents of these books cannot be taken literally, but they are a result of many centuries of collected writings and oral traditions, becoming an idealistic structuring of the historical situations and people involved in these stories. Several authors wrote the books at different times in history. The final writing and editing of the books took place around the sixth or fifth century before Christ, long after the events described took place.

Deuteronomistic History

Joshua, Judges, First and Second Samuel, and First and Second Kings, along with the Book of Deuteronomy, belong to a group of books known as *Deuteronomistic History*. Deuteronomistic History shares a common theme centered on the need for the people to remain faithful to the covenant established between God and the Israelites. If the nation remains faithful to God's covenant, God will protect it and lead it to victory in battles, but if the nation abandons the covenant, God will abandon it and allow other nations to plunder and conquer it. Although we use the term "the author" or "editor" throughout the book, the historical books are actually the result of many authors or editors.

Throughout the Old Testament, we read about the successes and tragedies endured by the Israelites. Besides invading the Promised Land, the Israelites themselves become victims of massive invasions throughout their history. After the death of Solomon, the Israelite kingdom broke into a northern and southern kingdom, with ten tribes forming the northern kingdom and the tribe of Judah forming the southern kingdom. The northern kingdom became known as the kingdom of Israel, and the southern as the kingdom of Judah.

Around 721 BC, the Assyrians decimated the northern kingdom, conquering the people, sending many of them into exile into other captured countries and bringing in people from captured countries to intermarry with the survivors. This mixed nation will later become known as Samaria. Some of the Israelites escaped from the invading Assyrians and fled south to the kingdom of Judah, bringing their stories and traditions with them.

Around 587 BC, the Babylonians invaded and destroyed the southern kingdom of Judah, carrying many of its inhabitants into exile to Babylon, an exile that lasted almost fifty years before the Judeans were allowed to return to their homeland. During this exile, the people of Judah kept their faith alive by sharing stories and messages gleaned from their life in Judah. Many of these stories were passed on orally, while some may have been written down.

Throughout their tragedies, the people recognized their failure to remain faithful to the covenant and their need to return to God. The Deuteronomistic author was able to gather ancient written traditions, the oral traditions of the people, and the stories and theological beliefs of the people from the northern and southern kingdoms. The result is a presentation of the history of the Israelite people, a presentation that contains true historical characters whose lives become magnified and idealized in the retelling.

Book of Joshua

The Book of Joshua follows upon the history found in the Book of Exodus, which speaks of the Israelites' escape from Egypt, their sojourn in the desert, and their preparation for entry into the Promised Land. The reader already met Joshua in the Book of Exodus as a military leader and an assistant to Moses, who chose to lead the people after the death of Moses. Just as the Lord was with Moses throughout the Exodus experience, so the Lord is with Joshua during the invasion of the Promised Land.

The theme of the Book of Joshua describes the conquest of the land of Canaan by Joshua and his army, a conquest promised by God to the Israelite ancestors. The book also speaks of a rapid conquest of the land, the battles and setbacks endured in this conquest, the division of the land among the twelve tribes, and a renewal of the covenant. As already mentioned in the Book of Deuteronomy, the success of the Israelites depends on their faithfulness to the covenant they made with God. When they abandon the covenant and worship other gods, God will abandon them.

One of the difficulties experienced by modern readers concerns the placing of a conquered city under the "ban," which was practiced in the Near East during the time of Joshua. The "ban" called for the total destruction of the conquered people, men, women, children, and livestock, thus avoiding any temptations the Israelites might have to worship the gods of the conquered people. The ban often resulted in burning the conquered city so that even the name of it would be wiped out.

Although the Book of Joshua gives the impression that the Israelites had conquered the Promised Land in a quick and successful manner, the Book of Judges and the books following show that the Israelites still had to fight the original inhabitants of the land. The land of Canaan contained a number of small tribes, not one large army that united the kingdom of Canaan. The conquest would demand a long period of fighting individual tribes before the Israelites could claim a large portion of the Promised Land.

Book of Judges

The Book of Judges does not refer to judges as we know them in a juridical sense today but to chosen leaders at particular times in the history of the Israelite nation in their early years in the Promised Land. Their continual battles are further proof that the Israelites did not sweep through the Promised Land with total victory. The judges include heroic or tragic leaders, some who were faithful to the Lord and some who were not. They were not leaders of the nation but leaders of a small portion of the people.

A common recurring theme in the Book of Judges is the Israelite abandonment of the covenant by turning their backs on God and worshiping other gods. When the Israelites turned against God, God abandoned them to their enemies. At this point, the Israelites would repent, crying out to God for help, and God would send a judge to lead them against their enemies. Although some of the stories of the judges may have come from written sources, most of them seem to come from an oral tradition. Many of them are obviously idealized images of heroic leaders.

A common repeated theme of the Book of Judges is: "In those days there was no king in Israel" (18:1). The book recognizes that God is the king of Israel, but it also prepares for the day when Israel would have a king. At the time of the final editing of the book, the editor already knew that Israel had a series of kings and had been conquered by foreign invaders.

Book of Ruth

The story of Ruth finds its place in the Bible from the first line of the book, which states: "Once back in the time of the judges...." This book becomes a link between the Book of Judges and First Samuel. It tells of a dedicated Moabite woman who is not an Israelite but who was married to a son of an Israelite woman named Naomi. When Naomi's son dies, Naomi directs Ruth to return to her people, but Ruth dedicates herself to the people of Naomi's ancestors.

Ruth will eventually become the wife of Boaz and the grandmother of David. Although she is not an Israelite, the Gospel of Matthew lists her among the ancestors of David and Jesus. The story shows God's universal concern for all people.

1 and 2 Samuel

Many commentators refer to Samuel as the last of the judges and a prophet. He comes upon the scene when there was still no king in Israel, and he will receive the call to choose a king for Israel. The books tell the story of the development of kingship in Israel and the challenges involved. Although Israel chooses kings, God still remains the king of the nation, and any sin, even those committed by a king, bring disaster upon the nation. The books of 1 and 2 Samuel present a story of Saul who fails as the first king and an idealized image of David.

The Book of Joshua (I)

JOSHUA 1—4

I command you: be strong and steadfast! Do not fear nor be dismayed; for the LORD, your God, is with you wherever you go (1:9).

Opening Prayer (SEE PAGE 16)

Context

Joshua, the new leader of the Israelites, orders the people to prepare to cross the Jordan and capture the land of Canaan. He reminds the tribes of Reuben, Gad, and the half-tribe of Manasseh of their promise to help the remaining tribes conquer the land beyond the Jordan. A woman named Rahab protects two Israelite spies sent to reconnoiter the land, and in return the Israelites promise not to harm her or her family. The spies bring news to Joshua that the people of the land fear the Israelites. When the time comes to capture the land, the Levitical priests lead the crossing by carrying the ark. As the priests enter the water with the ark, the water ceases to flow and all the people pass through the Jordan on dry land.

GROUP STUDY (JOSHUA 1—4)

Read aloud Joshua 1—4.

1:1–18 Joshua Leads the Israelites

The Book of Joshua immediately links with the end of the Book of Deuteronomy by stating that Moses had died and the Israelites needed a new leader. The author speaks of Moses as "the servant of the LORD" (1:1), a reference used for Moses only once, at the end of the Book of Deuteronomy: "So there, in the land of Moab, Moses, the servant of the LORD, died" (34:5). The term, "servant of the Lord," can only be used at the end of one's life, since it sums up a person's dedication throughout life. At the end of the Book of Joshua, the author will refer to Joshua in the same manner as "a servant of the LORD" to sum up his dedication to the Lord (Joshua 24:29).

Just as the Lord spoke to Moses during the Exodus, so Joshua became the one to whom the Lord speaks. At the end of Deuteronomy, the author stated that Moses, as he was dying, laid his hands on Joshua and was filled with the spirit of wisdom. Following the command of God given to Moses, the people became obedient to Joshua (see Deuteronomy 34:9). As though feeling a need to stress again that Moses is indeed dead, the author of the Book of Joshua has the Lord state, "Moses, my servant is dead" (1:2).

The Book of Joshua links with the Exodus by showing that the people who wandered through the wilderness have now reached the goal toward which they were aiming. The generation about to enter the Promised Land is not the same generation that left Egypt but is the generation born in the desert. The generation that left Egypt, with the exception of Joshua and Caleb, has passed away as a punishment for their grumbling against the Lord in the wilderness.

As the Lord promised, the Israelites will conquer all the lands upon which they will set their feet. This statement anticipates the battles the Israelites will undertake. The boundaries are described as expanding from the wilderness of the southern area of Canaan, to Lebanon on the east, to the Euphrates which is northern Canaan, and west to the Great Sea (the Mediterranean). No one will be able to resist Joshua for as long as he lives.

The author again links Joshua's role with that of Moses, showing that the Lord promised to be with Joshua just as the Lord was with Moses, never forsaking him. Joshua, like Moses, must remain strong and unfaltering so that he may lead the people to the possession of the land which God had promised to the Israelites as far back as Abraham. The Lord warned that the success of the people hinged on their obedience to the law given them by Moses. Throughout the Book of Exodus, when the people abandon the law given by the Lord to Moses, God punishes them for their disobedience.

In order to be successful, the people must not ignore even the smallest part of the law. To remain faithful to the law and attain their goal, they must recite it by day and night to be aware of its demands. The Lord again commanded Joshua to be strong and unwavering, moving ahead without fear and with confidence in the Lord, who promises to be with him wherever he goes. This command anticipated the conflicts ahead. In accepting his role of leadership, Joshua must dedicate himself to serving the Lord as Moses did, despite how difficult or impossible the opposition may appear to be.

Joshua performed his first act as the leader of the Israelites by commanding the officers of the people to go through the camp and order the people to prepare themselves with the supplies necessary to enter the Promised Land within three days. The officers of the people are those who were chosen to hold leadership positions within each area.

After addressing the officers of the people, Joshua had to remind the Reubenites, the Gadites, and the half-tribe of Manasseh of their promise to help in the conquest of the Promised Land. When these three tribes chose to remain in the land of Moab, Moses made them promise to send their warriors to fight with the Israelites when they crossed the Jordan and had to battle with the Canaanites. Their wives, children, and livestock could remain in the land given them by Moses, but the warriors were not excused from fighting for the land until the Israelites possessed it. The author does not describe the extent of land Israel possesses.

The three tribes, recognizing Joshua as their leader in place of Moses, declared that they will follow the orders of Joshua, doing all that he commanded and going wherever Joshua sends them. They profess that they will obey Joshua in the same manner that they obeyed Moses. They expressed their faith in Joshua by praying that the Lord would be with him as the Lord was with Moses, and they promised to kill anyone who did not obey Joshua's orders. The Israelites viewed Joshua's leadership as coming from the Lord.

2:1–24 Spies Saved by Rahab

Joshua secretly sent out two spies to reconnoiter the land and the town of Jericho. The need for secrecy shows that Joshua cannot trust everyone among the Israelites. The two spies traveled to Jericho, where they lodged at the house (apparently an inn) of a prostitute named Rahab. The king of Jericho received word that two men came to the inn the night before to spy on the land. The mission of the spies may have been twofold, namely to discover the weak points of the defenses of Jericho and to gain some help from the people of the land who were willing to support them. Since the king received word of their presence, they may have been openly asking for support.

The king of Jericho sent word to Rahab to bring to him the two men who were spying on the entire land. Rahab hid the spies among some stalks of flax on the roof of the house. The people used to spread stalks of flax out on their rooftops to dry in the sun after they soaked them. They would make a type of linen from them.

When the king's men came to the inn, Rahab feigned ignorance about the whereabouts of the two spies, saying that they did indeed come to the inn, but she had no more knowledge about them. She added that they left when it was time to close the gate to the city, and she urged the king's men to rush after them before it was too late. As soon as the king's men left, the gates of the city closed, thus effectively cutting off any hope of escape for the spies.

Rahab goes to the roof and speaks in a manner that clearly comes from the pen of the Deuteronomistic writer. Since she worked at an inn where many travelers would stop for rest, she could easily have learned about the exploits of the Israelites, but her speech, which is one of the longest by a woman in the Old Testament, appears to be structured by the author of the book. She expressed an awareness of the Israelites' escape from Egypt and how the Lord guided and protected them. She added that all the inhabitants of the land tremble with fear of the Israelites, a theme that the spies will bring back to Joshua.

In her speech, Rahab continued to describe how the Lord dried up the Red Sea for the Israelites when they escaped from Egypt and how they destroyed the two major armies of Sihon and Og, two kings of the Amorites. She stated that the Israelites' victories caused great dread among the people of the land and declares that the Lord, the God of the Israelites, is God in heaven above and earth below. In saying this, she is professing that there is one God as opposed to the many Canaanite gods. Although armies during the time of Joshua depended on their numbers and weapons, they still believed that their victories depended on the power of the gods. The people feared the God of the Israelites more than their army.

Rahab asked the spies to spare her and her family when the Israelites invade the land. She reasoned that just as she has treated the spies kindly, so they should treat her and her family kindly. In making this request, she asked for a sign that will allow her family to avoid destruction. The spies pledged on their lives that they would show kindness to her if she did not betray their mission, and they gave her a scarlet cord to place in the window of her house.

Some of the houses of Jericho were built into the wall of the city. Rahab lowered the spies down through a window in the wall with a rope, directing them to hide in the hill country for three days until their pursuers return home. The spies declared that they would consider themselves free of their oath if Rahab does not tie the scarlet cord in the window from which she was lowering them. She was to gather her family into the house, and if some were to leave the house during the invasion, they will be responsible for their own death. If, on the other hand, those in the house are harmed, their blood would be on the head of the spies.

The image of the scarlet cord recalled an image of the Passover. When Moses celebrated the first Passover, he directed the people to sacrifice a lamb and to paint the blood of the lamb on their doorposts. The angel of death would kill all the firstborn of those whose home did not have blood painted on the doorpost. The scarlet cord becomes a symbol of the blood on the doorpost. The Israelites, like the angel of death, would not kill anyone in the house where the red cord was tied in the window. Moses stated that all should gather together in a home to share the meal, and those not at home would face death. The spies warned that those in the family who left the house would cause their own death.

The spies hid in the hills for three days as directed by Rahab and traveled across the Jordan after their pursuers returned home. They brought the good news to Joshua, reporting that the Lord has put the land in their power and that the people are frightened because of the Israelites, most likely from all they have heard about them.

3:1–17 Preparing to Cross the Jordan River

The Israelites moved to a position near the Jordan River, where they remained for three days. Since some of the people never traveled over this land, the officers told the people to follow the Ark of the Covenant of the Lord (see illustration), which was being carried by levitical priests. The people are to remain approximately a little more than half a mile behind the ark. The movement of the ark and the distance of the people from it showed the importance and sacredness of the ark, which contained the text of the law and represents God's presence in the midst of the people as the one who is leading them.

The sacredness of the ark is further intensified when Joshua ordered the people to sanctify themselves. In the Book of Exodus, the author speaks of the people sanctifying themselves by washing their garments and to be ready for the "third day" when the Lord will come down on Mount Sinai (Exodus 19:10–11). On the third day, Joshua ordered the levitical priests to take up the ark of the covenant and cross in front of the people. The position of Joshua as the leader in place of Moses became more evident when he showed his authority over the levitical priests.

The Lord told Joshua to command the levitical priests to carry the Ark of the Covenant to the edge of the Jordan River. At this point, Joshua passed the words of the Lord on to the people, saying that their conquest of the inhabitants of the area will show that their God is a living God. Following Joshua's directions, the levitical priests stepped into the Jordan River, and just as the Red Sea no longer flowed when the Israelites crossed it in their escape from Egypt, so the Jordan ceased flowing when the levitical priests stepped into it. The image of the water standing as a heap reflects the image of the waters of the Red Sea standing as a mound in the Book of Exodus (see Exodus 15:8).

The story intensifies as the author describes the crossing of the Jordan that took place at the season of harvesting, that is, the time when the waters would be overflowing the banks. The waters stopped flowing for a great distance from a place named Adam, which is more than fifteen miles north of Jericho. This distance magnified the magnificent power of the living God. The nation crossed over on dry land as long as the levitical priests remained standing with the Ark of the Covenant in the middle of the Jordan. The people crossed over opposite Jericho, setting the scene for its capture.

4:1–24 Setting Up Memorial Stones

Upon entering the land promised to the Israelites by God, the Lord directed Joshua to choose twelve men, one from each of the twelve tribes, to take twelve stones from the riverbed where the priests were standing and to carry them to the site where they camped that night. The story of gathering the stones and setting them up became repetitious, apparently coming from the pens of various authors whose words were gathered together by an editor.

The place where the Israelites settled and set up the memorial stones received the name Gilgal, which means "circle." When their children would later ask about the meaning of the stones, the Israelites who crossed through the Jordan are to tell them that Israel crossed the Jordan on dry land, just as the Lord had done at the Red Sea. By this miraculous event, all people would recognize that the Lord is mighty and that all must fear the Lord, their God, forever.

Review Questions

1. Why did Joshua tell the people to recite the law daily? Explain the significance of this practice.

2. How does the red cord given to Rahab reflect the Passover event? Discuss.

3. What is contained in the Ark of the Covenant? Why do the levitical priests carry the ark to the edge of the Jordan River? Share and discuss important aspects of this event.

Closing Prayer (SEE PAGE 16)

Pray the closing prayer now or after *lectio divina*.

Lectio Divina (SEE PAGE 9)

Relax your body and maintain a posture of prayer (back straight, eyes shut, feet flat on the floor). This exercise can take as long as you want, but in the context of this Bible study, 10 to 20 minutes should be sufficient.

The meditations that follow are provided only to help group participants use this prayer form, but note that *lectio* is intended to bring one to a place of prayerful contemplation where the Word of God speaks to the hearer from his or her heart. (See page 9 for further instruction.)

Joshua Leads the Israelites (1:1–18)

The choice of Joshua to lead the people reminds us that all chosen leaders need prayers to fulfill their call to serve others. Like all leaders, Joshua did not lead the people by his own law but by the law given to the people by God. In 1 Timothy we read: "First of all, then, I ask that the supplications, prayers, petitions, and thanksgivings be offered for everyone, for kings and for all in authority, that we may lead a quiet and tranquil life in all devotion and dignity" (1 Timothy 2:1–2). Leaders within the Church and governments need prayers to serve with justice, humility, wisdom, and concern for those entrusted to their care. We pray that those chosen for leadership positions will, like Joshua, be faithful to the laws of the Lord.

✠ *What can I learn from this passage?*

Spies Saved by Rahab (2:1–24)

Joshua sent out spies to learn about the land of the Canaanites. It was a dangerous mission, and they almost lost their lives, but Rahab risked her safety to save them. We live in a secular society, and, like the spies, must learn how to live safely in a land where many attempt to live as though God's law of love and concern is not active. In the Gospel of Matthew, Jesus sends his disciples out on a dangerous mission and tells them, "Behold, I am sending you out like sheep in the midst of wolves; so be shrewd as serpents and simple as doves" (Matthew 10:16). In a secular society that puts material gains ahead of God, we have a great message to share by our manner of life. Jesus wisely tells us that in sharing that message, we must be as shrewd as serpents and as simple as doves. As we act in this manner, we will find people who are willing to support us in our endeavors.

✠ *What can I learn from this passage?*

Preparing to Cross the Jordan (3:1–17)

The Scriptures remind us that with God, all things are possible. When we read about the ark going into the Jordan and the water being held back, we can overlook the courage it may have taken for the people to cross the Jordan, seeing the walls of water heaped up on both sides of them and believing that it was not going to come crashing down on them. Sometimes, we can find ourselves called to trust God when all seems impossible or dangerous. But with God, we can dream the impossible dream and live a life of love of neighbor even if it causes us some discomfort or fear of retaliation. Just as the Israelites followed the Lord into the Jordan, so we can follow the Lord faithfully wherever it takes us.

✠ *What can I learn from this passage?*

Setting Up Memorial Stones (4:1–24)

In our world today, we have our memorial stones. The Vietnam Veterans Memorial Wall in Washington, D.C., is a memorial stone wall that reminds us of the bravery of soldiers who gave their lives for freedom. When Jesus gave us the Eucharist and said, "Do this in memory of me," he was establishing a memorial for future generations. The Israelites set up memorial stones so that generations to come could know what their ancestors did. We have our national and religious memorials to remind us of the good that went before us and the good that is expected of us.

✠ *What can I learn from this passage?*

INDIVIDUAL STUDY

This lesson does not have an individual-study section.

The Book of Joshua (II)

JOSHUA 5—24

Thus the LORD was with Joshua so that his fame spread throughout the land (6:27).

Opening Prayer (SEE PAGE 16)

Context

Part 1: Joshua 5—7 At Gilgal, all the male Israelites are circumcised and the Israelites celebrate their first Passover in the land of promise. For seven days, the priests carry the ark around Jericho, and on the seventh day, the people are to raise a loud noise and the walls of Jericho collapse. A short time after the conquest of Jericho, the Israelites are defeated at Ai. An Israelite named Achan had taken some plunder from the conquest of Jericho, and the Lord punishes the whole community. The Lord is appeased when Achan and his entire family are stoned to death.

Part 2: Joshua 8—24 The Israelites capture Ai. A tribe named Gibeonites later trick the Israelites into thinking that they had come from outside Canaan. The Israelite leaders make an oath not to kill them, but they soon discover that they were deceived. They make the Gibeonites slaves of the Israelites. Joshua leads a series of conquests against the Ammonite kings and kills some of the captured kings himself. Joshua seals the commitment of the Israelites to the Lord with a renewal of the covenant and dies shortly thereafter.

PART 1: GROUP STUDY (JOSHUA 5—7)

Read aloud Joshua 5—7.

5—6 Fall of Jericho

The kings of the Amorite tribes feared the Israelites when they heard of the miraculous drying up of the Jordan River that allowed the Israelites to cross on dry land. Those who entered the Promised Land had to live up to the demands of the covenant made between Abraham and the Lord by circumcising all the males. Circumcision was to be the external sign of the covenant. The Lord said to Abraham, "This is the covenant between me and you and your descendants after you that you must keep: every male among you shall be circumcised" (Genesis 17:10).

The Lord directed Joshua to make sharp flint knives to circumcise all the males of Israel. The editor added the phrase, "for a second time" (5:2) which is confusing and appears to be added by a later editor. In the Bible, a place is often named after the event which took place there. The name "Gibeath-haaraloth" means "Hill of the Foreskins." Those who came out of Egypt at the time of the Exodus were circumcised, but the second generation, who were born in the desert and who entered the Promised Land, were not. When all the males were circumcised, they remained in the camp until they recovered.

As a result of the circumcision of all the males, the Lord declared, "Today, I have removed the reproach of Egypt from you" (5:9). The reproach of Egypt referred not only to the time the previous generation spent in Egypt but also to their disobedience and murmuring in the desert. Because of the Lord's words to Joshua, the place named Gilgal is considered a sacred place.

The Israelites celebrated the Passover at Gilgal, on the plains of Jericho. It was fitting that they celebrated Passover at the end of their journey in the Promised Land, since it was celebrated by the Israelites right before their exit from Egypt (Exodus 12:1–28) when they were about to begin their journey. On the day of the celebration of the Passover in the Promised Land, the manna, which was given to feed the people in the wilderness, ceased, and the people ate of the produce of the land. The Promised Land, for the Israelites, was the land flowing with milk and honey, therefore the Israelites no longer had any need for manna.

As Joshua neared Jericho, he encountered someone with a drawn sword facing him. Joshua asked if he were one of his army or one of the enemy's. He was told that the armed one was neither, but was the commander of the Lord's army. When Joshua realized that he was in the presence of a divine being, he fell to the ground in worship. The divine one ordered Joshua to remove his sandals, since he was standing on sacred ground. This command corresponds with God's command to Moses from the burning bush when the Lord ordered Moses to remove his sandals, since he was standing on holy ground (Exodus 3:5).

The imagery of the armed one represented one who battles for the Lord, showing that the Lord is the true victor of the battles ahead. The Lord would fight for the Israelites as long as they remained faithful to the covenant but would leave them when the Israelites abandoned the covenant.

The number seven becomes significant in the fall of Jericho. The city was under siege, which means that the city was closed, with no one able to enter or leave. In the midst of this siege, the Lord informed Joshua that the Lord has delivered all of Jericho into his hands. The Lord directed Joshua to have the people and his soldiers circle the city one time each day for six days with seven priests carrying ram's horns ahead of the ark. On the seventh day, the seven priests with horns, the soldiers, and the priests with the ark marched around the city seven times. Joshua told the people to march around the city in silence until they hear the ram's horns and then they are to shout. On the seventh day, after walking around the city seven times, Joshua gave the command to shout. As they shouted and blew their horns, the walls collapsed and the Israelites attacked the city.

The author tells us that the city and all in it is under the ban. Being under the ban means that everything and everyone is to be destroyed. All belongs to the Lord, and no spoils are to be taken for anyone's personal good. If anyone takes anything, misery will come upon the whole Israelite community. All gold, silver, articles of bronze, or iron are holy and belong to the Lord and are to be put in the treasury of the Lord.

The killing of all the people may seem appalling to people of the world today, but when the Book of Joshua was written, this was a common practice. The reason the Israelites put Jericho under the ban was to avoid being influenced by survivors to worship false gods.

The only ones free of the ban were members of Rahab's family, because she saved the spies. Joshua directed the two spies to bring Rahab and her family out of the city. The Israelites burned the city and all within it. Joshua put a curse at the cost of his youngest son on anyone who would attempt to rebuild Jericho. This curse will be fulfilled later in the history of the kings, when, during the reign of King Ahab, Hiel rebuilds Jericho at the cost of his firstborn son and his youngest (1 Kings 16:34).

As a result of the fall of Jericho, the people recognized that the Lord was with Joshua, and he now became well-known throughout the land.

7:1–26 Achan's Offense

The author begins with a three-generation genealogy of an Israelite named Achan, who is identified as belonging to the tribe of Judah but breaks the covenant by confiscating booty that was under the ban. Since Achan was an Israelite, the whole community would suffer for his sin when they suffer a bitter defeat at a city named Ai.

Two spies—sent by Joshua to reconnoiter the land of Ai—returned to Joshua with a suggestion that he send only a force of about 2,000 or 3,000 to capture the city, since the enemy in the city consisted of only a few. Joshua sent 3,000 men, but they had to make a rapid retreat back to the camp after losing thirty-six men. The defeat destroyed the confidence of the Israelites.

As a sign of mourning this defeat, Joshua, with the elders, tore his garments and threw dust on their heads. They fell face down before the ark until the evening. Joshua asked why the Lord allowed this to happen. He feared that the Canaanites, who had trembled in fear before the Israelite army, would now become willing to engage the Israelites in battle and totally destroy Israel.

Joshua ended his prayer with the words, "What will you do for your great name" (7:9)? Not only would the defeat of the Israelites destroy the nation, but it would also point to a weakness of the God of Israel.

The Lord told Joshua that their defeat came because they had broken the covenant. One in their midst had taken some forbidden treasure from the battle at Jericho. The Lord directed Joshua to call the tribes together in the morning so that the Lord might designate who broke the covenant. That person and his family are to be destroyed by fire, with all his possessions, since he has committed a disgraceful crime in Israel. As each tribe came forward, the tribe of Judah was chosen by the Lord. When each clan within the tribe of Judah came forward, the Lord chose the ancestral tribe of Achan, and eventually chose Achan who admitted that he took a mantel, silver, and gold from the battle.

When the messengers Joshua sent to the tent of Achan found the hidden plunder, Achan, his family, and all his possessions were taken to Achor, a little more than seven miles south of Jericho, where they were stoned to death and their bodies and possessions burned. They covered the burnt remains with a large amount of stones. The name "Achor" means "trouble," which is appropriate since Achan brought trouble to the whole Israelite nation.

Review Questions

1. What does the fall of Jericho tell us about God's presence with the people?
2. Why does the Lord punish the whole Israelite community for the sin of Achan? Discuss.
3. Explain why the people of Joshua's day completely annihilated a city's people and livestock after battle.

Closing Prayer (SEE PAGE 16)

Pray the closing prayer now or after *lectio divina*.

Lectio Divina (SEE PAGE 9)

Relax your body and maintain a posture of prayer (back straight, eyes shut, feet flat on the floor). This exercise can take as long as you want, but in the context of this Bible study, 10 to 20 minutes should be sufficient.

The meditations that follow are provided only to help group participants use this prayer form, but note that *lectio* is intended to bring one to a place of prayerful contemplation where the Word of God speaks to the hearer from his or her heart. (See page 9 for further instruction.)

Fall of Jericho (5—6)

The idealistic story of the collapse of the walls of Jericho is a message about the rewards that will be granted those who trust the Lord. The Israelites fulfilled the requirements of the law, and they followed the Lord (the ark) to cause Jericho's downfall. Paul the Apostle often boasts of his weakness, but he is willing to trust the Lord. When he prayed to the Lord for help to overcome a weakness in his life, the Lord did not answer the prayer the way he wished, but the Lord told Paul, "My grace is sufficient for you, for power is made perfect in weakness" (2 Corinthians 12:9). The Israelite army may have been weaker than the army of Jericho, but the Lord brought them victory. The lesson for our life is to trust that the Lord helps us, even in our weakness and when the Lord seems not to hear our prayer. The grace of God is always at work when we pray.

✠ *What can I learn from this passage?*

Achan's Offense (7:1–26)

When some of Jesus' enemies asked if he paid taxes to the Roman conquerors, he responded, "Repay to Caesar what belongs to Caesar and to God what belongs to God" (Mark 12:17). Implied in his message is that the hearts of all human beings belong to God. We are made in the image and likeness of God. In ancient times, material possessions of a defeated nation belonged to God, unless God decreed otherwise. Achan's sin was not only greed, but the people of the era saw it as a type of blasphemy. He was stealing from God. Whenever we misuse God's gifts for sin, we are, in a sense, stealing from God. We will not be stoned to death for our sins, but we do hurt God's creation in some manner by taking for ourselves what belongs to God.

✠ *What can I learn from this passage?*

PART 2: INDIVIDUAL STUDY (JOSHUA 8—24)

Day 1: Conquest of Ai and the Gibeon Deception (8—9)

The Lord promised Joshua that he will successfully overcome Ai during this second attack and permitted the Israelites to take the spoils and livestock as plunder. Joshua sent several thousand warriors to the west side of the city as an ambush and set up his army to the north, facing the city of Ai. When the king and his army came to fight the Israelites on the north, the Israelites will feign a retreat, leading the whole army of Ai away from the city. As soon as the army was drawn away from the city, Joshua turned on the army of Ai and stretched out his javelin as a sign to those on the west side of the city to ravage and burn it to the ground. When the army of Ai saw the city burning behind them and the Israelite army now attacking them from the front and back, they lost heart and were totally annihilated. The king alone escaped and was captured.

Twelve thousand men and women of Ai, the entire population, were killed. The killing continued as long as Joshua held out his javelin. Following the directions of the Lord, the Israelites captured all the livestock and spoils of the city for themselves. Joshua hanged the king on a tree and left his body hanging from that evening until the next morning. The king was buried under a large pile of stones at the entrance of the city gate.

The victory at Ai came because the Lord fought with the Israelites. Another reason for the victory was that all of Israel's army was engaged in the battle, unlike the first attack, which consisted only of one part of the Israelite warriors and not the entire army. The Israelites would conquer as a nation, not as small segments of the nation.

In Deuteronomy, Moses ordered the Israelites to build an altar on Mount Ebal when they entered the Promised Land. They were to make the altar of stone which no iron tool had touched and coat the stones with plaster. On these stones was to be inscribed all the words of the law (see Deuteronomy 27:1–8). They were to offer burnt sacrifices to the Lord on this altar, which referred to offerings totally dedicated to the Lord to be entirely burnt. They were also to offer communion sacrifices which they were to eat with joy in the presence of the Lord. Moses also directed the Israelites to pronounce a blessing on Mount Gerizim for those who followed the law and a curse on Mount Ebal for those who disobeyed the law.

Joshua built an altar to the Lord at Mount Ebal, a place in the hill country. Following the directives given to Moses, Joshua made the altar of unhewn stones. The Israelites offered the burnt sacrifice to the Lord and the communion sacrifice as commanded. All were to stand on either side of the ark facing the levitical priests who carry it. Half of the people were facing Mount Gerizim and half Mount Ebal. The law was then read to all the people, with its blessings and curses.

The inhabitants of Gibeon knew that the God of the Israelites had given the land to them and that the Lord directed them to kill all the people of the land they conquered. They also knew that the Israelites were to treat aliens to the land with kindness, so they disguised themselves as travelers from a faraway land. In their weather-worn clothes and with their worn wineskins and dry bread, they approached the Israelites and claimed that they came to serve the Israelites. Without consulting the Lord, Joshua and the elders believed their story and made an oath to let them live.

Three days later, the Israelite leaders came to the city of Gibeon and realized that these people lived near them. Since they made an oath to let them live, they do not kill them. The Israelites grumbled against their leaders for making such an oath which they could not disobey. Since the Gibeonites deceived them, Joshua made them slaves to the Israelites, placing them as hewers of wood and drawers of water for the house of God. In offering sacrifices, the Israelites used wood for burning and water for dousing the fires. This type of work implied that the Gibeonites would carry out a number of lowly tasks for the Israelites.

Lectio Divina

Spend 8 to 10 minutes in silent contemplation of the following passage:

> A man came to the door of the rectory and asked the pastor for money for a meal and a motel room. The pastor gave the man money for food and called a nearby motel to arrange a room for the man to stay that evening. Later that evening, a woman called the pastor to report that she saw the man stopping by a liquor store and walking out with a

bottle to take with him to the motel. The pastor, saddened at the news, said to the woman that he did what he could for the man and he felt no regrets. He promised the Lord that he would help someone in need; he thought the man was in need, so he fulfilled his promise.

Like the Israelites who were confronted with the deception of the Gibeonites, those who strive to help others may be taken advantage of, but it is better to take a chance on helping a person who seems to be in need than to make the mistake of turning away someone who is in need.

✠ *What can I learn from this passage?*

Day 2: Further Conquests (10—21)

Gibeon was a city larger than Ai and lay just north of Jerusalem. The king of Jerusalem became anxious when he heard that his northern allies capitulated to the Israelites, and he called upon four other Amorite kings to join him in battle against Gibeon. As the kings laid siege to Gibeon, the Gibeonites sought help from the Israelites. The Lord informed Joshua that the Amorites would be delivered into his hands. Joshua marched all night with his army and overcame the kings with a surprise attack, killing many of the enemy and chasing the rest over a long distance.

While the Amorite kings and armies were fleeing, the Lord cast great stones from heaven on them, killing many of them. These stones may have been hail. Joshua prayed for the sun and moon to stand still while the Israelites slaughtered the Amorites. The story of the sun standing still is a well-known story in an idealized presentation of the battle. Some commentators attempt to explain it as the sun giving a longer period of light, others attribute the appearance of the moon as caused by an eclipse, and others maintain that it was a miraculous act of God. Whatever happened, the story is meant to show that the Lord was fighting along with the Israelites.

The author claims that the event of the sun standing still is recorded in the Book of Jasher, which may be an ancient lost book about the exploits of Joshua and others. The editor comments on the miraculous aspect of the story, declaring that there was never a day like this when the Lord obeyed the prayer of a human being and fought for Israel.

When Joshua heard that the five kings had fled into a cave, he ordered his men to roll a large stone over the entrance of the cave and to continue pursuing and killing the enemy. After pursuing the enemy, Joshua returned to the cave and brought out the kings. The kings were humiliated when Joshua directed the commanders to put their feet on the kings' necks. With a word of encouragement to the commanders to be brave and unwavering, Joshua killed the kings and hanged them on a tree until the next morning. He buried them in the cave in which they hid and placed large stones over the entrance.

Lectio Divina

Spend 8 to 10 minutes in silent contemplation of the following passage:

Joshua and the Deuteronomist historian lived in an era when they believed that complete annihilation of the enemy was God's will. Today we have Jesus' message to guide us, telling us that we must love our neighbor as ourselves. This means that even those who war against us are our neighbors. Mark Twain wrote a book titled *The War Prayer*, which prayed for a bloody conquest of the enemy. It is a satire that sees the incongruity of praying for a bloody end to the enemy. Many believe that Christ would see no problem in praying for victory, but the prayer should be a prayer for peace, where few of those engaged in the battle are killed.

✠ *What can I learn from this passage?*

A Note on the Conquests and Divisions of the Land
(found in 10:28—21)

Beginning in chapter 10:28 to the end of chapter 12, the editor lists a series of conquests in Southern and Northern Canaan, showing that the Israelites, with the help of the Lord, "conquered the entire land" and that he "left no survivors, but put under the ban every living being, just as the LORD, the God of Israel, had commanded" (10:40). The Israelites destroyed all the land and possessions except the spoils of the battle when the Lord permitted them to take these spoils. The series of conquests ended with a list of the conquered kings that amounted to "thirty-one kings in all" (12:24).

From chapters 13 to 21, the author lists the division of the land among the twelve tribes of Israel. The division begins with the Lord informing Joshua that although he is now old, a very large portion of the land still remains to be possessed. The land east of the Jordan was given to the Reubenites and Gadites and the half-tribe of Manasseh, who was the son of Joseph. The half-tribe of Manasseh is mentioned because Manasseh will receive another half beyond the Jordan.

The author mentions in detail the land given to these tribes. The Levites received no share of the land, but they were given land in the cities that they occupied as well as pasture lands for their herds and sheep. The Lord commanded the apportioning of the land to Moses. Caleb received the land promised to him by Moses when Caleb and Joshua were the only two in the desert who left Egypt and trusted that the Lord would help them conquer the Promised Land. The land is then apportioned to the tribes of Judah, the two sons of Joseph (Ephraim and the half-tribe of Manasseh). The sons of Joseph were too numerous for the land they received, so Joshua told them to take over the mountain region, which was a forest adjacent to their land.

For the seven remaining tribes, Joshua cast lots and divided the land among them, namely Benjamin, Simeon, Zebulun, Issachar, Asher, Naphtali, and Dan. In cases where the land was not enough for the number of people making up the tribes, the tribes would capture more land from the people of Canaan. The tribes gave Joshua the city he requested as commanded by the Lord.

The Lord ordered the Israelites to set up a city of refuge for those who unintentionally or inadvertently killed another. The killer could flee to one of these places of refuge and plead his case before the elders at the city gate, who could then allow him to live in their midst. When the high priest died, the killer was free to return to the place where he originally lived. The author names these cities of refuge.

The Levites were not given a portion of the land, but they received cities from each of the tribes in which to reside with a place to pasture their animals. The author then names the cities each of the tribes gave to the Levites.

Day 3: Eastern Tribes Released (22:1–34)

As already mentioned, the Reubenites, the Gadites, and the half-tribe of Manasseh settled on the eastern side of the Jordan. Joshua commended them for remaining faithful to their promise to help the Israelites conquer the Promised Land. Now that the Lord had settled the others as promised, the eastern tribes may return to their tents. The only warning they received is that they remain faithful to the covenant. The warriors from these tribes had amassed an abundance of spoils from plundering and Joshua told them to share their treasures with their allies.

After the three eastern tribes returned home, they built a large altar facing the land of Canaan. Believing that this large altar symbolized worship of a false god, the other tribes prepared for battle with them. They sent a delegation with Phinehas, son of Eleazar the priest, and representatives of the remaining tribes, expressing their fear that if the tribes across the Jordan had turned away from the God of the Israelites, the whole community would be punished.

The three eastern tribes asserted that if they have rejected the God of gods, they would be punished. The altar was not an altar for sacrifice but an altar to witness that they remained faithful to the one true God worshiped by the Israelites beyond the Jordan. If future generations would believe that the three tribes did not cross the Jordan because they rejected the God of the Israelites, this altar will stand as a witness of the eastern tribes' unity with the other tribes of Israel. The delegation returned home, pleased to pass the good news on to the community across the Jordan.

Lectio Divina

Spend 8 to 10 minutes in silent contemplation of the following passage:

> The Israelites settled their differences with the eastern tribes by speaking with them and learning that they built an altar as a witness of unity between the eastern and western tribes. Early in the twentieth century, Christian denominations often spoke against each other and rarely with each other, strongly stressing those points that divided them. In the mid-twentieth century, the attitude began to change as the different denominations sat down together and shared their beliefs. To their surprise, they discovered that they agreed on a large number of theological points concerning Christ and his message, although many theological differences still remained. Open dialogue, like that of the eastern and western tribes in the past and that of the different denominations in the present, leads to peace, understanding, harmony, and love.

✠ *What can I learn from this passage?*

Day 4: Joshua's Farewell (23—24)

The scene moves to years later. The author, continuing to recognize that the Lord has been the one to lead the Israelites to victory, states that the Lord now gives them rest from their enemies. Joshua, who is old, gathers together the Israelites and reminds them how the Lord, who fought for them, helped them defeat all the nations in the land.

In speaking of the allotment of the land as a heritage given to each tribe, Joshua encouraged them to trust that the Lord will drive all enemies from their land. For their part, they were to remain faithful by observing all that the Lord commanded them, neither worshiping false gods nor mingling with those who worship false gods. Joshua called on the Israelites to acknowledge that all that the Lord promised had been fulfilled. If they turn away from the Lord, the Lord will reject them, and their enemies would totally drive them out of the land they now possess.

Joshua told the people that he is "going the way of all the earth" (23:14), which means that he is dying. He urged them to acknowledge that all that the Lord promised had been accomplished from the time the Lord chose Abraham down to their invasion of the Promised Land. He warned them that just as God has fulfilled every promise, so God will also fulfill all the threats made against them if they fail to remain faithful to the covenant.

Joshua challenged the people to decide if they will follow the Lord of the Israelites, the gods of the lands they left behind or the gods of the land they conquered. He declared that he and his household will serve the Lord. In response, the people asserted that they too will follow the Lord who led them from slavery and fought for them in the Promised Land. Joshua warned the people that God is a holy and passionate God and that it will be a challenge for the people to remain faithful, but the people remained unyielding in their commitment to the Lord.

Joshua ended by renewing the covenant of the Lord with the Israelites. He wrote statutes and ordinances in the book of the law of God at Shechem and set up a large stone in the sanctuary as a witness to the covenant. He sent the people to the land allotted them as a heritage for their tribe.

Just as the author refers to Moses as a "servant of the Lord" at the time of his death (see Deuteronomy 34:5), the author likewise calls Joshua "servant of the LORD" at his death (see 24:29). The book ends with a reference to the burial of Joseph. In doing this, the author links Joseph with Joshua. Just as the saga of the Israelites' progress from Egypt toward the Promised Land began with Joseph inviting the family of Jacob into Egypt (see Genesis 47), so it ends in the Promised Land with the death of Joshua. When Joseph was dying, he made his sons take an oath that they would bring his bones from Egypt (Deuteronomy 50:25). Like Joshua, Joseph lived to the age of 110.

Joshua was buried in the land of his heritage. The Israelites remained faithful to the Lord during Joshua's lifetime and that of the elders who knew of all that the Lord had done for the nation. The bones of Joseph were buried at Shechem in a plot of ground purchased by Jacob (Genesis 33:18–20). The author tells us that this was the heritage of the descendants of Joseph. The Book of Joshua ends neatly with the death of the high priest Eleazar, the son of Aaron, thus concluding the lives of all who led the people during the time of Joshua. Eleazar was buried on a hill in the mountain region of Ephraim, which was given to his son, Phinehas.

The name of Phinehas begins the new era of the Israelites' sojourn in the Promised Land.

Lectio Divina

Spend 8 to 10 minutes in silent contemplation of the following passage:

At the end of their lives, Moses and Joshua received recognition as servants of the Lord. The stories reserved this praise of them after their death, implying that they remained faithful servants throughout their lives. God established a creation in which God needs all of us as servants of the Lord, no matter what work or ministry we perform in the world. God needs the person performing a minimal, unknown task for the human community as much as God needs leaders to govern and guide the human family. Whatever our work or whatever the condition of our life, God needs us. God needs us to perform our tasks well, as servants of the Lord.

✠ *What can I learn from this passage?*

Review Questions

1. How did Joshua's army conquer the army of Ai?
2. Why were the Gibeonites willing to become vassals of Israel?
3. What caused the tribes on the western side of the Jordan to fear when they saw the altar erected by the eastern tribes?
4. Why does Joshua make a new covenant with God for the people right before he dies?

The Book of Judges (I)

JUDGES 1–14

Hear, O kings! Give ear, O princes! I will sing, I will sing to the LORD, I will make music to the LORD, the God of Israel (5:3).

Opening Prayer (SEE PAGE 16)

Context

Part 1: Judges 1—5 The Book of Judges begins with a double introduction. The first introduction, from 1:1 to 2:5, speaks of the failure of the Israelites to drive out all the Canaanites, and 2:6 to 3:6 depicts a recurring cycle of the people's unfaithfulness, repression, repentance, and deliverance. Since the main part of the book begins with 3:7, the reader may choose to read or skip the double introduction, which is set to grayscale in this commentary.

From 3:7 on, the story of the judges unfolds. Among the first three judges mentioned is Ehud, who killed Eglon, the king of the Moabites. The next story concerns Deborah, a prophet and judge, and Barak. Barak defeats a Canaanite army, and a general named Sisera flees, but he is killed by a woman named Jael. Deborah then sings a song of victory.

Part 2: Judges 6—14 The next judge, Gideon, defeats the Midianites. Abimelech, a son of Gideon, becomes the judge after Gideon, but God punishes him for his evil ways and he is killed by a woman. A judge named Jephthah defeats the Ammonites, but he has to sacrifice his daughter because of a foolish oath he made before going into battle.

PART 1: GROUP STUDY (JUDGES 3:7—5)

Read aloud Judges 3:7—5.

Double Introduction
(participants may elect to skip chapters 1 through 3:6)

The first introduction (1—2:6) stresses the importance of the tribe of Judah and hints at the dominance of Judah at the time the author wrote his section of the Deuteronomistic History. Judah called upon his brother-tribe of Simeon to join him in battle against the Canaanites, promising in turn to battle with the tribe of Simeon when it attempts to capture the territory allotted to it. Judah was successful in defeating the Canaanites and a tribe known as the Perizzites, killing thousands of the enemy. The chapter speaks of Judah gaining one victory after another against the Canaanites in various areas of the Promised Land. The Lord was with Judah in these victories.

The Benjaminites were not able to overcome a group known as the Jebusites from Jerusalem, so both groups lived together in Jerusalem. In the history of Israel, Jerusalem was not an Israelite possession until David later captured it. The tribe of Manasseh was not able to clear the land of the Canaanites, although they forced some of them into slavery. The remaining tribes were also not successful in driving the people out of the areas allotted to them.

A messenger of the Lord warned the people that the Lord never breaks a covenant with them, but they did not listen to the Lord and, as a result, the Lord did not fight with them. The Lord had warned them earlier that the inhabitants of the land would become a trap for them and their false gods shall ensnare them. When the people heard this, they wept aloud. They had abandoned the Lord and they wept when they encountered the consequences.

The second introduction (2:6—3:6) links with the end of the Book of Joshua, repeating essentially the ending passage of Joshua 24:29–31. It is the more appropriate introduction to the Book of Judges, since it introduces the cycle of abandoning the Lord, crying out to the Lord, and experiencing deliverance from the Lord. When later generations arose who did not know the Lord and were not aware of all the Lord had done for them, the Israelites worshiped the Baals, false gods of the land.

Because of their sinfulness, the Lord abandoned the Israelites and allowed the enemy to plunder and destroy them and their possessions. When they cried out under the oppression of their enemies, the Lord raised up judges to save them. After the death of the judges, however, they did worse than before in their worship of false gods.

Because the people abandoned the Lord, the Lord refused to clear away any more nations Joshua left unconquered when he died. The Lord allowed the enemies of the Israelites to remain in the land to test the Israelites and to see if they would remain faithful to the Lord. The Israelites settled among the people of the land, intermarried with them, and served their gods.

3:7–31 The First Three Judges

Although the judges may appear to be saviors of the whole nation of Israel, they seem to be more like saviors of a small portion of Israel. The first judge introduced is Othniel, and his story follows the cycle of sin, a cry for help, and deliverance. When the Israelites abandoned the Lord and served the Baals, the Lord sold them into the power of the king of Aram. They were no longer a special possession to be protected by the Lord. When the people cried out for help, the Lord raised up as their savior Othniel, the son of Caleb's youngest brother, Kenaz. The Lord's spirit came upon Othniel, and he (Othniel) judged Israel. The Lord delivered the king of Aram into his power and as a result, the land enjoyed a period of forty years of rest.

Later, the Israelites returned to their evil ways, and the Lord gave strength to Eglon, the king of Moab. With the Ammonites and Amalek as allies, he defeated Israel and took possession of the city of Palms. The Israelites served him for eighteen years. When the Israelites cried out to the Lord, the Lord chose Ehud, who was left-handed and belonged to the tribe of Benjamin. The author is using a play on words here, since the name Benjamin means "son of the right hand." Ehud was chosen for the task of bringing the yearly tribute from the Israelites to Eglon. In preparation for this visit, he made a two-edged dagger a foot long and strapped it under his clothes on his right thigh.

Although the author does not explain the need to stress that Ehud was left-handed and that he attached the dagger to his right thigh, some commentators deduce that this was a ploy to sneak the dagger past the guards, while other commentators maintain that it was meant to be the source of a surprise attack on Eglon. When Ehud would enter the chamber of the king, the guards would most likely search him, but they would search his left thigh for a dagger, since a right-handed person would ordinarily reach across his body to his left to grasp a weapon. The guards would most likely not notice that Ehud was left-handed and would not think of checking his right side.

The author made the story more graphic as he described how very fat Eglon was. After the presentation of the tribute took place, Ehud dismissed the troops who carried the tribute. He told the king that he has a secret message for him. The king sent his attendants away, and Ehud tells the king that he had a message from God for him. When the king came close, Ehud drew the dagger from his right side with his left hand and thrust it into Eglon's fat belly up to the hilt. The fat closed over it and Ehud left it in the body. Ehud left the upper room, locked the doors, and left the palace. When the servants arrived, they believed that Eglon was "easing himself," that is, relieving himself. After waiting a period of time, the servants took the key, opened the door, and found the king dead on the floor.

The delay in finding the king allowed Ehud time to escape. He later gathered together the Israelites and led them in a battle against the Moabites.

He told the Israelites that the Lord delivered the Moabites into their hands. The author stated that about 10,000 Moabites were slaughtered. No one escaped. The Israelites have a rest from battle for eighty years.

The author makes a short reference to Shamgar, who slew 600 Philistines, adding that Shamgar was also a savior for Israel. Shamgar was the first of the minor judges, which is a reference to the shortness of the stories where there is little said about them.

4—5 Deborah and Barak

After the death of Ehud, the Israelites again turned against the Lord, and the Lord sold them into the power of a Canaanite king named Jabin. Although the author names Jabin at the beginning of this part of the narrative, the central figure in the following story was Sisera, a general in Jabin's army. Jabin's army tyrannized the Israelites with his 900 iron chariots, the most advanced weapons of the day. The Israelites, who again realized that the Lord had abandoned them because they abandoned the Lord, cried out to the Lord for help. The Lord sent them help in the person of Deborah, the wife of a man named Lappidoth.

Deborah does not appear on the scene as a warrior but as one who judges between God and the people. Like many judges of her day, her judgment took place under a specified tree. Deborah, acting as a prophetess as well as a judge, summoned a leader named Barak and informed him of the Lord's command that he lead 10,000 men in a march against Sisera at Mount Tabor. Barak refused to march unless Deborah traveled with him. She agreed, but she prophesied that he will not gain glory for the expedition, but that the Lord will sell Sisera into the hands of a woman.

When Sisera received the news of Barak's march, he went to fight him, but the Lord threw Sisera and his chariots and men into a panic, and the whole army of Sisera was cut down by the sword. The scene recalls an earlier scene in the Book of Exodus when the Lord looked down upon the chariots and horsemen of the Egyptians who were thrown into a panic when the Lord crushed them in their attempt to cross the Red Sea in pursuit of the Israelites (Exodus 14:24–25). In the midst of the panic, Sisera dismounted from his chariot and fled on foot to the tent of a woman named Jael, who, like Shamgar in the previous chapter, was not an Israelite. She welcomed

Sisera into her tent as though she were caring for a friend and covered him with a rug.

Sisera presumed that cunning Jael was an ally, and her concern supported this idea. He requested water to quench his thirst, and she gave him milk. He told her to stand at the entrance of the tent and to answer "no" to anyone who asks if there is someone here. When Sisera fell into a deep sleep, Jael took a tent peg and a mallet and, crawling quietly to Sisera, drove the peg through his temple and down to the ground, killing him.

When Barak arrived, Jael told him that she would lead him to the man he was pursuing. Barak went in the tent and found Sisera dead with a peg through his temple. On that day, the Lord humiliated the Canaanite king, Jabin, for the Israelites. The king was overcome with the power of the Israelites. Deborah warned Barak earlier that a woman would gain the glory for the victory, and so it happened. Leaders sought glory for winning battles, but it would be Jael, not Barak, who would receive the praise for the death of Sisera.

In chapter 5, Deborah sings her song which many commentators believe is one of the most ancient songs in the Scriptures and one that was written before the events taking place in chapter 4, inspiring the story found therein. Chapter 4 interprets in prose form what is found in Deborah's song, and it adds more details than those found in the song.

The song, which is directed to the Lord, begins with a dramatic image of the Israelites rising up and singing praise to the God of Israel. It pictures the earth as shaking, with the heavens pouring down rain, an image of a visitation from the Lord. The canticle sings of the mountains streaming from the Lord of Sinai, the Lord God of Israel. Then Deborah rose to the occasion, a mother in Israel, a phrase which may indicate Deborah's leadership role. Deborah praises those dedicated leaders who assisted in the battle. In chapter 4, the author speaks of Naphtali and Zebulun as joining in the battle, but the canticle of Deborah sings of other nations who helped and berates those that did not.

Although the canticle praises Barak, it offers special praise to Jael, a tent woman, who gave milk to Sisera and killed him. In the poem, the manner of death differs from that found in chapter 4. In both chapters, Jael uses a peg and a mallet, but the canticle pictures Sisera as sinking at her feet, not as sleeping.

The scene changes as Deborah pictures the mother of Sisera at home looking down from her window through the lattices, wondering what is keeping Sisera's chariot from arriving. She, along with the wisest of princesses, judged that he must be dividing the spoils of battle such as dyed cloths. And the canticle ends with a reflection on the destruction of the enemies of the Lord, while those who love the Lord are pictured as the rising sun. As found after the stories of previous judges, the author ends this episode by saying that the land was at rest for forty years.

Review Questions

1. Explain how the story of Ehud sets an example of the role judges play in Israel.

2. How does the role of Deborah differ from that of Ehud? Make a list of some differences and share within your group.

3. Why are there two different explanations of Jael's killing of Sisera? Discuss.

Closing Prayer (SEE PAGE 16)

Pray the closing prayer now or after *lectio divina.*

Lectio Divina (SEE PAGE 9)

Relax your body and maintain a posture of prayer (back straight, eyes shut, feet flat on the floor). This exercise can take as long as you want, but in the context of this Bible study, 10 to 20 minutes should be sufficient.

The meditations that follow are provided only to help group participants use this prayer form, but note that *lectio* is intended to bring one to a place of prayerful contemplation where the Word of God speaks to the hearer from his or her heart. (See page 9 for further instruction.)

The First Three Judges (3:7–31)

Ehud, the first of the major judges, leads the Israelites, the people of God, to victory over the tribe of Moab by killing the Moab leader. Christians are sometimes called to battle in defense of a country or in defense of an innocent party. At times such as these, Christians do not kill out of vengeance nor do they destroy innocent people. Saint Joan of Arc is an example of someone who led an army in battle and was later canonized because she believed she was fighting for the Lord. Killing innocent people in the name of God is wrong, but there are times when a Christian is called to kill in a just war. It is always a difficult choice.

✠ *What can I learn from this passage?*

Deborah and Barak (4—5)

In the days of the judges, being killed by a woman was a great humiliation for a warrior. In the story of Deborah and Barak, two women play leading roles, one as a prophetess and guide, and the other as the one to kill a great general. The story may be God's way of revealing to people that women have a place in freeing Israel from its enemies. In the world today, there are times when women must fight for the right to be recognized as equal to men. In the Gospel of Luke, Mary is sitting at the feet of Jesus, listening to his words. In Jesus' era, Jewish women never sat at the feet of a rabbi, learning from him. Jesus, however, defends Mary's action when Martha complains. Jesus says, "Mary has chosen the better part and it will not be taken from her" (Luke 10:42). Jesus confirms that women have a right to learn, as men do. God created men and women equal to each other.

✠ *What can I learn from this passage?*

PART 2: INDIVIDUAL STUDY (JUDGES 6—14)

Day 1: The Saga of Gideon (6—8:28)

The Israelites again chose their evil ways over the Lord, and, for seven years, the Lord abandoned them to the power of the Midianites and other raiding parties who ravaged the Israelites, who were now settlers in the land. To the Israelites, the number of raiding parties appeared to be like a swarm of locusts. The Israelites suffered to such an extent that many of them fled to dens and caves in the mountain. The raiders would attack after the Israelites completed sowing their crops and would destroy whatever produce they could find.

When the Israelites cried out to the Lord for help, the Lord sent a prophet, a messenger of the Lord, who attempted to turn their thoughts back to the Lord, the one who cared for them from the time they escaped from Egypt, but they would not listen to him. The messenger of the Lord visited a man named Gideon who was grinding the wheat in a wine press in an attempt to save it from the raiding parties. When the messenger told Gideon that the Lord was with him, Gideon immediately challenged the messenger, asking why these evil things are happening to them if the Lord is with them. The messenger of the Lord addressed Gideon as a "mighty warrior" (6:12), a hint about his future accomplishments.

So, in this story, the messenger of the Lord became the Lord, as happened with Jacob when he wrestled with an angel all night and in the morning realized that he had been wrestling with the Lord (Genesis 33:23–32). Gideon, however, was not aware of the identity of his guest. When Gideon learned that the Lord wanted him to lead the people, Gideon objected; he states that he is the poorest in the land and the most significant person in his family, but the Lord promised to be with him. Gideon's objections bring to mind the call of Moses before the burning bush, where Moses offers objections to the Lord's choice (Exodus 3:11–14; 4:10). Just as the Lord gave signs to Moses that the Lord was with him (Exodus 4:1–9), so Gideon sought signs from the Lord.

Gideon begged the Lord not to leave until he brought out an offering for the Lord. He prepared a young goat and some flour in the form of unleavened cakes and brought the offerings out under the terebinth tree, placed them on a rock and poured out broth which he himself prepared. When the messenger of the Lord touched the offerings, a fire erupted from the rock and consumed the offerings. At this, the messenger of the Lord disappeared. Gideon, suddenly realizing that his visitor was the Lord, became frightened because he had seen the Lord face to face. The Lord told him not to be afraid and assured him that he would not die, since the people of ancient times believed that if they saw God they would die.

Throughout the story, Gideon appeared to waver and show fear as he followed the Lord's commands. The Lord ordered him to destroy the altar of Baal and the image of the female goddess, but Gideon, fearing for his life, destroyed the altar to Baal at night, when no one would see him.

The following morning, when the people found the altar to Baal destroyed and the image of the female goddess destroyed, they learned that Gideon had done this. The people demanded that Gideon's father bring him out, but his father asks if they should act in place of their god. He warned that anyone who takes action in place of their god would be put to death. He told them to let their god destroy him. Gideon received the name Jerubbaal, because his father said, "Let Baal take action against him." This name will appear in place of Gideon in the following chapters.

When the Midianites, Amalekites, and the Kedemites threaten the land of Manasseh, Gideon gathered an army from among some of the tribes of Israel, from the tribes of Asher, Zebulun, and Naphtali. Gideon again sought signs from the Lord. He challenged the Lord to make a fleece become moist overnight without the ground around it becoming moist. When the Lord granted his request, he made a second request for the next night. He requested that the ground around the fleece become wet without the fleece becoming wet. The next morning, he found the ground moist and the fleece dry.

Then the Lord challenged Gideon further by reducing the number of his warriors. The Lord directed Gideon to send home those who were afraid or fearful. Twenty-two thousand men left. The Lord tested Gideon even further and told him to lead his men down to the water and have them drink. Those who lap up the water like a dog are to remain, while those who cup the water in their hands and drink in that manner are to be sent home. Those who remained numbered 300. With such a small number, there will be no doubt that the Lord is the true conqueror of the enemy.

That night, the Lord directed Gideon to sneak down into the camp of the enemy with an aide named Purah. As they crawled close to two soldiers, they hear one of them speaking about a dream he had the night before. It was a dream about a round loaf of barley bread which rolled into the camp, came to a certain tent, struck it, turned it upside down, and the tent collapsed. The other soldier concluded that this can only be the sword of Israel, and he fears that God has delivered Midian and the whole camp into Gideon's power. Gideon returned to the camp, told his warriors about the discussion he overheard, and declared that the Lord has delivered Midian and all in the camp into his power.

Gideon divided his men into three companies, giving of them horns and empty bottles with torches inside them. He directed his men to follow his example, telling them that he will go to the edge of the camp, and, when he blows his horn, they are to do the same all around the camp and cry out, "For the Lord and for Gideon." When they carried out their mission, they caused a panic in the camp, leading the soldiers to fight each other and fleeing, but the Israelites pursued them with soldiers from Naphtali, Asher, and Manasseh. Gideon sent messengers to the Ephraimites who joined in the battle and were ready for the enemy, many of whom were killed. The Ephraimites killed many and presented the heads of two major Midian leaders to Gideon.

The Ephraimites became angry, asking Gideon why he did not bring them into the battle from the beginning. Gideon reminded them that the Lord delivered the princes of Midian into their hands. He asked what more could be done in comparison with that. Their anger subsided.

Gideon continued to pursue Zebah and Zalmunna, the kings of Midian. Since Gideon's men were exhausted and hungry, he came to the princes of Succoth and asked for food. The princes mocked them, telling them that the Israelites have not yet conquered the enemy, and it appeared that such a conquest would not happen. When they refused to give food to Gideon's army, Gideon said that when he captured his prey, he will return to destroy the people and the camp. The people of Penuel also refused to give food to Gideon, and he threatened them in the same way.

Zebah and Zalmunna had a remaining force of about 15,000 men, since they had lost 120,000 men. Gideon captured Zebah and Zalmunna. He then returned and destroyed the princes of Succoth and slaughtered the people. He also destroyed the tower of Penuel and killed the people in the city, likewise killing Zebah and Zalmunna.

Because of his victory, the people wanted him to become their ruler and to pass the rule onto his son, grandson, etc. Gideon refuses to rule them and states that his son will not rule as a king over them. The Lord is their ruler. The desire for a king becomes a dominant issue for the remainder of the Book of Judges.

Gideon requested that each one of the people give him a ring from the spoils they collected. He spread his cloak on the ground into which each one threw a ring. Gideon made an ephod of a god out of the gold and placed it in his city. He may have meant this ephod to be an image of the one true God, but to make such an image would be a sin. All Israel prostituted themselves in worshiping this ephod, and it became a snare to Gideon and his household. During the lifetime of Gideon, the land had rest for forty years.

Lectio Divina

Spend 8 to 10 minutes in silent contemplation of the following passage:

When God deals with the enemies of Gideon, God wants to prove that the God of the Israelites is the only true and powerful God. Because of this, God sends Gideon into battle with an outnumbered handful of men who route the enemy. As Christians, we believe that God is always acting in our life in some manner. God does not control us to the point that we are puppets and God the puppeteer pulls the strings, directing every action of our lives. But we believe that God inspires us to act in certain ways and gives us the strength and guidance we need. Whether or not we follow God's unseen promptings often depends on our free will to accept or reject God's grace in our lives.

✠ *What can I learn from this passage?*

Day 2: Leadership of Abimelech (8:29—10)

After the death of Gideon, the Israelites returned to the worship of false gods. Gideon had seventy sons and many wives, and from a concubine he had a son named Abimelech. Abimelech sought to become king, and he killed his seventy brothers in his father's house by hiring unsavory men and outlaws for seventy pieces of silver taken from the temple of the Baal. The Lords of Shechem and Beth-millo made Abimelech king, and his only surviving brother, Jotham, stood at the top of Mount Gerizim and cried out in a loud voice.

Jotham shouted out a canticle story about trees being asked to become a king over the other trees. The olive tree refused to give up its rich oil to rule over the other trees. The fig tree refused, asking if it must give up its sweet fruit to hold sway over the other trees. The vine also refused, asking if it must give up the wine that cheers the gods and human beings to rule over other trees. The buckhorn agreed that it would rule over these trees if the trees are asking in good faith. It invites the other trees to come and rest under its shadow, but if not in good faith, then let fire come from the buckhorn and devour the cedars of Lebanon. The cedars of Lebanon represent the people who are seeking a king.

Jotham applies this parable to the people of Shechem. If they have elected Abimelech in good faith because he was their kin, then they have acted in good faith, and they can rejoice in Abimelech as king while he likewise may rejoice in serving them. But if they have not acted in good faith, let fire come forth from Abimelech upon the lords of Shechem and from the lords of Shechem to devour Abimelech, thus destroying each other.

After three years under Abimelech's rule, God put an evil spirit between Abimelech and the lords of Shechem to repay the violence done to the seventy sons of Jerubbaal. The lords of Shechem wanted to avenge the brothers and plotted to ambush Abimelech.

They placed their trust in a man named Gaal, whom they believed would destroy Abimelech. So they harvested the grapes to make wine for a festival and all went to the temple of their gods, where they celebrated together and cursed Abimelech. Gaal boasted that he would depose Abimelech. A ruler of the city reported to Abimelech about Gaal's boast, stating that Gaal was stirring up the people of the city against him (Abimelech).

Throughout the night, Abimelech set up an ambush outside the city. Gaal went out to meet Abimelech in battle and suffered a terrible defeat. When the army marched out against the army of Abimelech, Abimelech rushed to take over the gate while the rest of his army fought out in the field. Abimelech fought throughout the day and successfully captured and demolished the city, spreading salt over the land so that it would make the soil useless.

The evil of Abimelech is shown more forcefully as the lords of the city went into a crypt in the Temple. Abimelech had his army carry brushwood, lay it around the crypt, and set it on fire so that a thousand men and women perished. He went on to another city where the people fled into a well-built tower in the middle of the city. When he came close to set it on fire, a woman cast the upper part of a millstone down on Abimelech, fracturing his skull. The upper part of the millstone is the part that is ordinarily used by the people to ground against a larger, lower stone. Even as he lay dying, Abimelech showed concern for his reputation. He did not want people to say that a woman killed him, so he asked his attendant to spear him through "and he died" (Judges 9:54). With the death of Abimelech, the Israelites left for their homes.

The author states that the Lord repaid the evil Abimelech had done to his father in killing his seventy brothers. The curse of Jotham, the son of Jerubbaal, was fulfilled in Shechem as punishment for the wickedness of the people.

Lectio Divina

Spend 8 to 10 minutes in silent contemplation of the following passage:

Abimelech suffers the greatest humiliation in his day—killed by a woman! When he was near death, he was foolishly worried about his reputation. There was a rich and proud man who set aside a large sum of money for a large statue of himself to be built after his death. He requested that the statue be placed in front of a town library for which he paid to have built. The town's people were overjoyed at his gift of the library, and they willingly took the money he left for his statue, had it cast, and placed in front of the library.

Within five years, a major factory in town closed its doors and in the next few years, many people had to leave town for work elsewhere. Eventually, the town deteriorated, with stores and the library closing. Thirty years later, a man and his young son were driving through the ghost town, and the boy looked at the decaying statue and asked, "Who is that?" The father answered, "I don't know!" Christians believe that our greatest monuments are not the statues we leave behind after we die but the people whose lives we have touched.

✠ *What can I learn from this passage?*

Day 3: The Sage of Jephthah (11—12)

Two minor judges follow upon the story of Abimelech: Tola, who judged for twenty-three years, and Jair, who judged for twenty-two years. After the period of these two judges, the Israelites sinned against the Lord again by worshiping false gods. Because of their unfaithfulness, the Lord abandoned them to the Ammonites and others invading from the east. The powerful Ammonites—a semi-nomadic people—crossed from the eastern side of the Jordan to plunder Gilead, the area allotted to the tribe of Gad. They also fought against Judah, Benjamin, and Ephraim, throwing Israel into a panic and in need of a great leader.

As usual, the Israelites cried out to the Lord, but the Lord pointed to all the times they were saved. This time the Lord refused to act. They begged the Lord, and to show their sincere commitment, they abandoned their foreign gods and served the Lord. This sets the stage for the next judge of Israel.

The Lord chose Jephthah to be the new judge of Israel, despite his uncertain beginnings. He was the undesirable son of a prostitute whose brothers cast him out from the tribe, assuring him that he would not inherit anything from his father Gilead. Jephthah led a group of unsavory men in raids on the people. When the Ammonites attacked Gilead, the elders begged Jephthah to lead them, saying that if he defeated the Ammonites, he would be accepted as their leader. The outcast could hardly pass up the opportunity to become the leader of the people.

Before engaging the Ammonites in battle, messengers ran back and forth between Jephthah and the Ammonites. Jephthah asked why the Ammonites wanted to invade the land of the Israelites. The Ammonites pointed to a past event, when the Israelites, on their journey through the wilderness, captured land from the Ammonites. Jephthah responded that the Israelites wanted to pass through the land peacefully, but the Ammonites chose to block them and engaged them in a battle lost by the Ammonites. Jephthah accused the Ammonites of unjustly choosing to fight the Israelites, and he calls upon the Lord to decide the outcome.

The spirit of the Lord came upon Jephthah, who made a foolish vow to the Lord, saying that if the Lord granted him victory against the Ammonites, he will sacrifice to the Lord the first one who came out the door when he returned home. In Israel, animals would often be housed on a lower level where they could freely meander in and out of the house. Jephthah believed that he would sacrifice a precious animal to the Lord. Unfortunately, after he inflicted a defeat on the Ammonites and returned home, his daughter came out to meet him, playing a tambourine and dancing, celebrating his victory.

Jephthah's joyful victory became a disaster, knowing that he must fulfill his vow and sacrifice his only child. When he explained to his daughter the vow he made, she agreed that he must fulfill his vow to the Lord who granted him victory, but she requested that she and her companions be permitted to go to the mountains to weep for her virginity. Israel believed that a woman who died without a child was cursed by the Lord. At the end of the two months, she returned and Jephthah did what he had vowed. This was the beginning of a custom in Israel for the women to go out for four days each year to mourn the daughter of Jephthah. Jephthah already had the assurance that the Lord was with him, therefore he did not need to make a vow to the Lord if he were victorious. Jephthah, like most of the judges, did not always make virtuous choices.

The tribe of Ephraim complains against Jephthah, saying that he went out to fight against the Ammonites without their help. Jephthah responds that the Ammonites were pressing in on the land and he sent to Ephraim for help, but they refused. Ephraim threatens to destroy and burn Jephthah and his family, so Jephthah engages them in battle, forcing them to turn and flee. Jephthah stations his men at fords in the river that the escaping Ephraimites had to pass. The soldiers would question those who passed the fords whether or not they were Ephraimites. When the escaping soldiers answered that they were not, then Jephthah's soldiers would say the word "Shibboleth." If they used the Ephraimite tongue saying "Shibboleth," the soldiers would hack them down, for they were not able to pronounce the word properly. Because of this, 42,000 Ephraimites lost their lives.

Jephthah judged Israel for six years and was buried in Gilead. Three minor judges followed after Jephthah. Ibzan, who judged Israel for seven years, committed the sin of marrying outside the family and having his sons do the same. He was buried in Bethlehem. Elon, who judged for ten years, died and was buried in the land of Zebulun. Abdon, who judged for eight years, was buried in the land of Ephraim. The authors tell us little about these minor judges except that they had many sons and seemed to prosper. There is no mention about the Israelites abandoning God during this period of the minor judges.

Lectio Divina

Spend 8 to 10 minutes in silent contemplation of the following passage:

The story of Jephthah teaches a lesson about foolish oaths and the need to trust God. God already promised Jephthah that he would succeed, but he added the foolish oath that he would sacrifice whoever came out to meet him when he returned home. As a result, he had to sacrifice his daughter. The story teaches that whenever we are tempted to make a promise to God, it is helpful to choose a promise that will be kept. If we break the promise we make to God, we do not commit a sin but must simply begin again. If we are going to make a vow, then we choose a spiritual guide to help us discern the wisdom of such a move.

✠ *What can I learn from this passage?*

Day 4: The Saga of Samson (13—14)

The saga of Samson is a story of a hero who does not lead an army, but one who acts alone against the dreaded Philistines, who would plague the Israelites well into the period of the kings. The Philistines were sea people who migrated to Canaan around 13 BC, less than a century after the Israelites crossed the Jordan under the leadership of Joshua. They settled on the western coast of Canaan and moved inland in the centuries ahead.

The story of Samson is one of the best-known stories in the Book of Judges. Although he is considered a hero by the Israelites for his single-handed slaughter of a large number of Philistines, his weaknesses identify him as a careless and fickle Israelite. The story begins with the usual message that the Israelites did what was evil and, as a result, the Lord delivered them into the power of the Philistines for forty years.

The birth of Samson follows the theme of many great births in the Scriptures, namely a period of his mother's barrenness followed by the conception of a child. An angel appeared to Samson's mother, the wife of Manoah of the tribe of Dan, and predicted that she will bear a son and that he is to be subjected to the nazirite vow, which meant that he could drink no wine or beer, eat nothing considered unclean, and not have his hair cut. Not mentioned here but found in the Book of Numbers where the nazirite vow is explained, those who take this vow shall be forbidden to touch a corpse (see Numbers 6:1–21). The Book of Numbers implies that a person makes this vow for himself, but in this case, the angel decreed it for Samson. The angel promised that he will save the Israelites from the powerful Philistines.

Manoah's wife reported to her husband the visit of the angel. Since she had the child with the nazirite vow already existing in her womb, she had to obey some demands of the vow, namely avoiding wine and unclean foods. Manoah prayed that the Lord would guide him and his wife in raising a child with such a lofty destiny. His prayer was answered when the angel of the Lord appeared to Manoah and his wife, and the angel reminded them that Manoah's wife must follow the directives of the Nazirite vow.

Manoah offered hospitality to the angel by suggesting that Manoah kill a goat for a meal. The angel, instead, urged him to sacrifice the goat to the Lord, which is what Manoah does. In the end, as the angel disappeared in the smoke from the sacrifice, Manoah and his wife suddenly realized that they have received a visit from the Lord. Manoah panics, fearing that they will now die since they have seen the Lord face to face. His wife assures him that the Lord would not let them die.

Samson met a Philistine woman whom he wanted to marry, but his parents asked him to find someone among their kinfolk. The author adds that the Lord was using the marriage as an opportunity for Samson to eventually act against the Philistines. In the vineyards of the area of Timnah, Samson encountered a young lion and tore it apart with his bare hands. A short time later, when he was going to Timnah to marry the woman, he went into the vineyard to look at the remains of the lion and discovered that a swarm of bees made use of the carcass to make honey. He scooped out the honey and ate it on his journey. He later shared some with his parents without telling them where he found it.

Samson celebrated his marriage with a great feast, according to the custom of the day. The Philistines give him thirty men to be his companions, perhaps assuring themselves that Samson would be pleased with such attention or to keep an eye on him. Samson used this occasion to challenge the companions with a riddle, saying that "out of the eater came food, out of the strong came sweetness" (14:14). If the companions solved the riddle in seven days, Samson promised to give them thirty linen tunics and thirty sets of garments, a rich prize in those days.

Samson's thirty companions apparently became concerned after three days and, on the fourth day, they asked Samson's wife to trick him into telling her the answer to the riddle. For seven days, Samson's wife wept, telling him that he must not love her since he would not give her the riddle's answer. Samson finally relented, gave her the answer, and she passed the answer onto the thirty companions. On the seventh day, the men said, "What is sweeter than honey, what is stronger than a lion" (14:18)?

Samson knew that they received their answer from his wife. He told them that if they had not plowed with his heifer, they would not have solved the riddle. In other words, if they had not connived with his wife (heifer), they would not have solved the riddle. Samson, however, had to pay as he promised, so he killed thirty men, stripped them of their garments, and gave the garments to those who answered his riddle. In anger, he returned to his own family, and Samson's wife was married to the companion who was his best man.

Lectio Divina

Spend 8 to 10 minutes in silent contemplation of the following passage:

God blessed Samson with great power, but Samson was as strong-headed as he was strong-bodied. He also took his great strength for granted, using it for his own gain or to randomly kill the Philistines. He was a strong man out of control. Like Samson, we have gifts given to us by God. We are not bodily as strong as he was, but God chose us for a certain part of God's plan. Saint Paul tells us that we are the body of Christ, and each of us has a unique gift, but none of us possesses all the gifts (1 Corinthians 12). From Samson's mistakes, we can learn the importance of using our gifts wisely and as God desires.

✠ *What can I learn from this passage?*

Review Questions

1. How does Gideon's story show that God is the one to win the battle and not Gideon's army?

2. Why is Abimelech so concerned about the news spreading that a woman killed him?

3. Explain why Jephthah's oath of sacrificing his daughter was foolish.

4. Do you think it was right for Samson's mother to honor the nazirite vow for Samson even before he was born?

The Books of Judges (II) and Ruth

JUDGES 15—21 and RUTH 1—4

Wherever you go, I will go, wherever you lodge, I will lodge. Your people will be my people, and your God, my God. Where you die, I will die, and there be buried (Ruth 1:16b–17a).

Opening Prayer (SEE PAGE 16)

Context

Part 1: Judges 15—16 Delilah tricks Samson into telling her that the source of his power is his hair. When Delilah cuts his hair, he loses his strength and is placed in prison. His hair grows back, and he is able to topple the supporting pillars of the Temple, which kill Samson and a large number of Philistines.

Part 2: Judges 17—21 and Ruth 1—4 Danites persuade the Levite priest of a man named Micah to leave the house of Micah and become their priest instead. In a town named Gibeah, a Levite's concubine is raped by the townsmen and dies. The Levite cuts her body into twelve pieces and sends each part to rally all the Israelites to fight against the town in the area of the Benjaminites. The Benjaminites lose a battle against the Israelites and had to capture women from other tribes to assure their future.

Ruth, a daughter-in-law of the Israelite, Naomi, goes with her mother-in-law after Ruth's husband dies. She marries Boaz and gives birth to Obed, who was the father of Jesse, who was the father of David.

PART 1: GROUP STUDY (JUDGES 15—16)

Read aloud Judges 15—16.

15—16:3 Samson Defeats the Philistines

Samson returned to the Philistine town to seek his wife, but he received the news that she was given in marriage to his best man by his wife's father, who thought that Samson hated her to the point of not returning. In response, Samson caught 300 fox and tied them tail-to-tail, setting torches on them and sending them into the standing grain of the Philistines. In response, the Philistines burned Samson's wife and her family to death. Samson slaughtered many of the Philistines in anger, and other Philistines went after Samson.

In the meanwhile, the Philistines threatened to harm the tribe of Judah if they did not turn Samson over to them. Because of the Philistine's threat against Judah, Samson allowed the people of Judah to tie him up and turn him over to the Philistines, but after the Philistines took him away, the spirit of the Lord gave Samson the power to break the ropes. He took the jawbone of an ass and killed a thousand Philistines. The name of the place was *Ramath-lehi,* which means "jawbone."

Samson, thirsty and weak, complained to the Lord, asking if he were to be conquered by the uncircumcised Philistines. The Lord split a rock and water flowed out for Samson to drink until his strength returned. The name of the place is *En-hakkore,* which means "the spring of the crier."

Samson went to be with a prostitute. The people of the town where he stayed planned to ambush Samson in the morning when the gate of the city opened. But at midnight, Samson tore the gateposts loose, put them on his shoulders, and carried them for close to forty miles.

16:4–31 Samson and Delilah

Samson again fell in love, this time with a woman named Delilah. The Philistines offered her money if she could find out the source of Samson's strength. When she asked Samson for the secret of his strength, he told her that if they bind him with seven fresh bowstrings that have not dried, he will grow as weak as anyone else. With men in hiding, she tied him as he said and shouted that the Philistines were upon him. Samson leaped up and snapped the bowstrings.

Delilah accused him of mocking her, and Samson told her that if they bind him with new ropes with which no work had been done, he would be weak like everyone else. While he slept, she tied him with new ropes and shouted that the Philistines had come. Samson leaped up and snapped the ropes. The same happened a third time when he told her that if she weaved the seven locks of his hair into a web and fastened them with a pin, he would become weak. When she shouted that the Philistines were upon him, he awoke and pulled out the loom and the web.

She finally asked how Samson could say he loved her when his heart was not hers. She complained that he mocked her three times in not telling her the truth. Finally he told her that if his hair is shaved, he would be weak. After he fell asleep, she had the locks of his hair cut off, and when she shouted that the Philistines had come, he was too weak to defend himself. The Philistines captured him and gouged out his eyes, as was done to prisoners to keep them from rebelling. They placed him in slavery with the task of pushing a giant grinder to grind grain. His hair began to grow during his imprisonment.

The Philistines gathered to celebrate a feast in honor of their god Dagon. Part of the celebration consisted of celebrating the imprisonment of Samson and making a spectacle of him. Samson requested an attendant to place him between the two pillars that supported the Temple. The roof of the Temple and the Temple itself were filled with men and women. Samson grasped the two columns, prayed to the Lord for strength, and pushed aside the pillars, causing the Temple to collapse and bringing death to more people than Samson had killed throughout his life. Samson died in the collapse of the Temple. He judged for twenty years.

Review Questions

1. Why did the Philistines war against the Israelites?

2. Why is the biblical story of Samson and Delilah so intriguing for many readers? Share your insights within the group.

3. How does the story of Samson differ from the stories of the other judges? Discuss.

Closing Prayer (SEE PAGE 16)

Pray the closing prayer now or after *lectio divina*.

Lectio Divina (SEE PAGE 9)

Relax your body and maintain a posture of prayer (back straight, eyes shut, feet flat on the floor). This exercise can take as long as you want, but in the context of this Bible study, 10 to 20 minutes should be sufficient.

The meditations that follow are provided only to help group participants use this prayer form, but note that *lectio* is intended to bring one to a place of prayerful contemplation where the Word of God speaks to the hearer from his or her heart. (See page 9 for further instruction.)

Samson Defeats the Philistines (15—16:3)

The story of Samson reminds us that the gifts we have received from the Lord are not given to us because we are virtuous people but for the common good. Samson was the champion of Israel sent to fight against the Philistines. The Lord gives a person gifts for the common good, even if that person is not a virtuous person. A healer who used the healing powers God gave him for his own wealth and prosperity admitted to a friend that God gave him the gift of healing, not because he was worthy but for the good of people who needed healings.

✠ *What can I learn from this passage?*

Samson and Delilah (16:4–31)

Samson's love for Delilah leads him to reveal the source of his strength and to be captured by the Philistines, who gouge out his eyes. In a sense, he was blinded by his strength, but now, in his weakness, he is able to recognize a final call to destroy many of the Philistines and be a hero to the Israelites. When his hair grows back, the Lord gives him his strength back and he destroys the Temple and a multitude of Philistines. The encouraging message of the story is that the Lord's plans can be fulfilled, even when those chosen are weak and they misuse the gifts that they receive.

✠ *What can I learn from this passage?*

PART 2: INDIVIDUAL STUDY (JUDGES 17—21 AND RUTH 1—4)

Day 1: Micah and the Levite (Judges 17—18)

From chapter 17 to 21, the Book of Judges no longer speaks of judges chosen by God but of people who have lost leadership. Four times, the author writes, "In those days, there was no king in Israel" (17:6; 18:1; 19:1; 21:25). On two occasions, the author adds the words, "everyone did what was right in their own sight (eyes)" (17:6; 21:25).

The situation in these last chapters in the Book of Judges may have taken place at an earlier time between the periods when Joshua died and before God designated certain people as judges. During that time, the tribes established their own loose form of leadership under the elders of the people. These elders were not individuals but groups of men whose wisdom was accepted by the people. Without any established leadership, the people had to do "what was right in their own eyes," which meant that attitudes about God and worship could vary from tribe to tribe.

An example of someone who did what was right in his own eyes was a man named Micah. Micah stole 1,100 silver pieces from his mother, and his mother, not knowing who stole the silver pieces, placed a curse on the person. Micah, highly religious and superstitious, became frightened about being cursed, so he admitted that he stole the silver pieces. His mother lifted the curse and instead blessed him for admitting his theft.

Micah's mother decided to dedicate the silver to the Lord, and she gave 200 pieces of silver to the silversmith to have an idol made. The idols in those days could symbolize an image of a false god or an image of the God of the Israelites. The silversmith would make the idol out of wood and overlay it with silver. According to the Law of Moses, the Israelites sinned in making an image of the God of the Israelites. It is not clear whether the idol is one of a false god or an idol meant to symbolize the one true God. But both types of images are forbidden by the Law of Moses.

Micah's mother left the idol with Micah, who had a shrine in his house. Micah made an ephod (priestly garments) and a teraphim (household idols), and placed them in the shrine. Since he believed that he should have a priest with the shrine, he appointed his son his priest due to the lack of a descendant of Aaron. In Micah's era, this practice of choosing a male from among one's sons to act as a priest was an acceptable practice in the absence of a priest from Aaron's line.

A young Levite was traveling from Bethlehem when he stopped at the home of Micah. Micah begged him to remain and become a father and priest to him in place of his son. So Micah believed that the Lord would now bless him since he had a Levite as his priest.

In Joshua's allotment of land to the twelve tribes of Israel, the tribe of Levi did not receive an allotment of land, but they were to serve as a priest for the tribes. Only those who were offspring of Aaron were the levitical priests. Others in the tribe of Levi who were not priests had the duty of caring for sacred places and preparing the sacrifice, but they did not sacrifice it on behalf of the people, except in the absence of a priest from the line of Aaron. Since they served each tribe by offering sacrifice and caring for the sacred areas, tribes would offer a place for the descendants of Levi to live, providing sustenance and an income as well.

In the meanwhile, the tribe of Dan searched for a heritage, which means a place for the current members of the tribe and all descendants. Although the author of Judges states that the Danites did not receive an allotment of land, the Book of Joshua stated that the tribe of Dan did receive its allotment and had to capture more land since the allotment was too small for the number of people in the tribe (Joshua 19:40–48). Although Dan did receive an allotment, they may not have been able to capture their allotted territory and now had to go in search of a land in which to settle.

When the Danites sent five robust men to find a place for the them to settle, they were passing the house of Micah when they heard the voice of the Levite. They asked the Levite to consult the Lord to see whether their journey would be successful. The Levite informed them that the Lord will grant them a peaceful journey. Afterward, the scouts continued their journey to a town named Laish and found people living in an area that was remote from other nations. When the scouts discovered that the people of Laish were a quiet and trusting people, apparently referring to their vulnerability, they returned to their camp and reported that Laish will be easy to conquer and that the Lord has placed Laish in their hands.

The Danites sent 600 men to capture the land. On their journey, the five scouts spoke about the young Levite and his priestly garments, household idols, and an idol overlaid with silver. The army stopped at the Levite's home and asked if he wished to serve one man or a whole tribe. The young Levite took the priestly garments, the household idols, and the silver-covered idol and joined the Danites. Micah pursued them in an attempt to regain his possessions, but when the Danites threatened him and his family, he abandoned the quest, realizing that the Danites were too powerful for him.

The Danites easily captured the city of Laish, destroyed it with all its inhabitants, built a new city, and named it Dan after their ancestor who was one of the twelve sons of Jacob. The Danites set up an idol for themselves and chose Jonathan, the son of Gershom, who was the son of Moses, to be their priest. This Jonathan is apparently the young Levite who agreed to leave Micah and join them. The descendants of Jonathan were the priests for the Danites until the captivity of the northern kingdom centuries later by the Assyrians around 721 BC.

The author who wrote this portion of the Book of Judges already knew that King Jeroboam I of the northern kingdom, the kingdom of Israel which had split from Judah, established Dan as one of the two sites for worship in the northern kingdom. The other was Bethel. Jeroboam feared that if the people kept traveling to Jerusalem to worship, they would eventually rejoin the southern kingdom, the kingdom of Judah. A golden calf became the center of the temple at Dan. The people may not have worshiped the golden calf, but they saw it as a visible place where the invisible God rested, much like the footstool of the ark where the Lord, although not visible, rested between two images of angels.

Lectio Divina

Spend 8 to 10 minutes in silent contemplation of the following passage:

The people of the Old Testament era realized the need for a priest to offer sacrifice to God on their behalf day after day. The Levite and his offspring were extremely important to the Danites. The offering of these priests, however, was the prelude to the greatest sacrifice in God's creation. Jesus came as a new high priest who did not offer animal sacrifice but offered himself as the one sacrifice that suffices and brings salvation to all. The Book of Hebrews says of Christ: "He had no need, as did the high priests, to offer sacrifice day after day" but "he did that once for all when he offered himself" (Hebrews 7:27). Central to Catholic worship is the celebration of the Eucharist, which is not a new offering each time it is celebrated but an ongoing sharing in the death, resurrection, and ascension of Jesus, which has taken place once and for all.

✠ *What can I learn from this passage?*

Day 2: Outrage and Unity (Judges 19—21)

Chapter 19 again notes that in those days, there was no king in Israel. It was during this period that a Levite took a concubine from Bethlehem of Judah who abandoned him and returned to her father's house. When the Levite went after her, the girl's father joyfully welcomed him, knowing that he would take the concubine back with him. Late on the fifth day, the man left with his concubine and servant. As evening drew on, the Levite and his companions were passing near Jebus (Jerusalem), and the servant wanted to spend the night there, but the Levite did not trust the people of the area, so they traveled to Gibeah and, as was the custom in ancient times for travelers, they sat in the town square until an old man came by and invited them to lodge with him for the night.

While they were enjoying the elderly man's hospitality, some scoundrels beat on the door, demanding that the man turn over the man so they could have their way with him. Since hospitality was so important and women mattered little in the society, the old man offered his virgin daughter and the concubine to the crowd. When the crowd refused his offer, the old man grabbed the concubine and pushed her out the door. Throughout the night, they raped and abused her. In the morning, the concubine collapsed at the entrance of the house of the old man.

When the Levite opened the door and found her, he showed no pity and ordered her to get up. Since she could not answer, he placed her on his donkey and journeyed home. At home, he cut the dead concubine up into twelve pieces and sent them to the tribes of Israel to avenge the crime. When the tribes received this gruesome message, all of them, from Dan to Beersheba, gathered at a place named Mizpah. From Dan to Beersheba meant from north to south. They numbered about 400,000. The Levite informed them about all that has happened at Gibeah of the tribe of Benjamin, and they decided to war against Gibeah with as many as ten percent of the men of Israel.

Before warring against the tribe of Benjamin, the tribes of Israel formally requested that the tribe of Benjamin turn over the culprits who raped the concubine. The Benjaminites refused and mustered 26,000 swordsmen and 700 left-handed men especially skilled with slingshots. The tribe of Judah was chosen to lead the attack against the Benjaminites. The tribe of Judah was apparently viewed as a powerful force blessed by the Lord (see Judges 1:2).

The first two battles left the Israelites thoroughly defeated by the Benjaminites. Weeping over their enormous loss of life and the two defeats, the Israelites went to Bethel to seek the Lord's advice. The high priest and the ark were at Bethel. The author names Phinehas, who was the son of Eleazar, the son of Aaron, and was the priest when Joshua was alive. The author could simply be using the name of Phinehas to refer to the offspring of Phinehas, just as the Israelites wept over the killing of their brother Benjamin, meaning the offspring of Benjamin.

At Bethel, the Lord told the Israelites that their third attack against the Benjaminites would be successful. In this battle, the Israelites chose a strategy used by Joshua in his battle at Ai (see Joshua 8:1–29). They had some men lie unseen on one side of the army of the Benjaminites. The Israelite force facing the Benjaminites fled as the Benjaminites charged them. This deceived the Benjaminites into thinking that they were winning the battle, and the Benjaminites remaining in the city rushed out to join their forces in their apparent conquest of the Israelites, leaving the city unprotected.

The army of Israel that had hidden in the vineyards entered the city and set it aflame. When the retreating Israelites saw the smoke of the burning city, they turned to confront the attacking Benjaminites. The Benjaminites suddenly realized what had happened and went into a panic. Many of them attempted to escape, but the Israelites caught and killed them. The Israelites destroyed everything in the city and destroyed other cities of the Benjaminites, killing all the men, women, children, and livestock.

The men of Israel had taken a vow at Mizpah that none of them would give their daughters in marriage to the Benjaminites. The victors went to Bethel and wept that the tribe of Benjamin would become extinct without women to marry.

The Israelites also made a vow that anyone who did not go to battle with them would be put to death. After a roll call, they realized that the people of the town of Jabesh-gilead had not engaged in battle. So they raided the city and spared only the virgins in the city, who numbered 400. The reason for the vow and the slaughter was most likely due to the idea that Israel was a community that was successful when all were involved. It had religious as well as military overtones. They brought the women to the camp at Shiloh, in the land of Canaan. They gave these women to the Benjaminites as wives, but 400 was not enough.

The elders devised a plan to keep the tribe of Benjamin from becoming extinct. They knew that the people of Shiloh celebrated the Feast of Tabernacles with dancing, so they instructed the men of Benjamin to hide in the vineyard, and when the women came up to dance, they were to take them captive and bring them to the camp of the Benjaminites. When the men of Shiloh complained to the elders, the elders encouraged them to release their daughters, since the people of Shiloh did not break the vow by giving their daughters to the Benjaminites, but instead the Benjaminites took the women by force.

The Benjaminites flourished, rebuilt their cities, and the tribes continued as before. The Book of Judges ends with the telling words, "In those days, there was no king in Israel; everyone did what was right in their own sight" (21:25). These words prepare the way for the Book of Samuel and the establishment of a kingdom in Israel, but first comes the story of Ruth, grandmother of David.

Lectio Divina

Spend 8 to 10 minutes in silent contemplation of the following passage:

> The author illustrated the ripple effect of sin in the story of David and Bathsheba. In this story, the ripple effect of sin appears again with greater consequences. The lust of the men of the town lead to the death of an innocent woman, to the need for revenge on the part of the Levite, and to the arrogant pride of the Benjaminites protecting the sinners. This continues with a bloody conflict against the other tribes of Israel and almost causes total annihilation of the tribe of Benjamin. In our own era, we witness how pride, greed, revenge, or the quest for power can lead to world wars. Jesus knew how one sin leads to another, so he told his followers not to seek revenge but to forgive seventy-times seven times, which means always (Matthew 18:21–22).

> ✠ *What can I learn from this passage?*

Day 3: Ruth's Story (Ruth 1—2)

The Book of Ruth begins in the time of the judges, when a great famine ravaged the land. A man named Elimelech traveled from Bethlehem of Judah with his wife, Naomi, and his two sons, Mahlon and Chilion, to the plateau of Moab, a land blessed with rain and produce, more so than in his native place. They were Ephrathites from a small area in Bethlehem of Judah, not to be confused with a town named Bethlehem in the north. The prophet Micah writes some eight centuries before Christ, "But you, Bethlehem-Ephrathah, least among the clans of Judah, from you shall come forth for me one who is to be ruler in Israel" (Micah 5:1). The ruler in Israel is a reference to King David.

Sometime after their arrival at the plateau of Moab, Elimelech died. The two sons of Naomi married Moabite women, one named Orpah and the other Ruth. Ten years after Naomi and her sons settled on the plateau of Moab, her sons died and Naomi decided to return to Bethlehem. She urged her daughters-in-law to return home to their "mother's house," which means to their home. The term "mother's house" could refer to the woman's part in the house or to the place where marriages are arranged. In the Song of Songs, the lover speaks of bringing the beloved to the house of the mother of the lover (see Song of Songs 3:4). When she tells them to go home, Naomi prayed that they will find the same kindness from the Lord that they had shown to her and her family.

Naomi's distraught daughters-in-law refused to leave her, but Naomi insisted, saying that she had no more sons in her womb, and even if she did, would they be willing to deprive themselves of a husband until her children were old enough to have a child with them? This is a reference to a Levirate marriage found in the Book of Deuteronomy which commanded that when a woman's husband died, his brother shall have a child by the woman and the firstborn son shall bear the name of the deceased brother (see Deuteronomy 25:5–10). Orpah wept and kissed her mother-in-law farewell, but Ruth declared that where Naomi goes, she will go, and she will make Naomi's people her people, and Naomi's God her God. Naomi and Ruth traveled together to Bethlehem.

At the beginning of the barley harvest, they arrived in Bethlehem. Upon their arrival the excited people of Bethlehem greeted them, and Naomi expressed her bitter experiences since they have left; she told them not to call her Naomi, which means sweet, but Mara, which means bitter.

Because of her marriage to Elimelech, Naomi gained a powerful relative named Boaz. As a relative, Boaz had the duty of caring for Naomi in some manner. According to the Book of Leviticus, the harvesters were not to reap to the very edge of their fields, but they must leave the gleaning for the poor (Leviticus 19:9–10). Because she and Naomi were among the poor, Ruth decided that she would go and glean wherever she was permitted. She happened to glean in a section owned by Boaz. Boaz arrived and inquired about the girl gleaning on his field. The overseer said that she was the Moabite who arrived with Naomi and that she had worked unceasingly all day without rest.

Although Boaz was the owner of the land, he showed a friendly regard for his workers in addressing them and receiving a blessing from them.

He immediately welcomed Ruth among the women who gleaned and instructed her not to go to other owners but to go where the women gleaned on his land. He treated her with great deference, inviting her to drink when thirsty. When Ruth prostrated herself and asked why he was treating her with such favor, he answered that he had already heard about her kindness to Naomi and her choice to live among people she did not previously know. He hoped that she would experience the blessings of the God of Israel, who brought her to them for refuge. The reference to the God of Israel as the one who protected her was a reference to Ruth's early words when she declared that Naomi's God would be her God.

Boaz showed her special favors as he invited her to come and eat, dipping her bread into the sauce, which is a manner of sharing in the friendship of the host. He gave her more grain to eat than she needed. After the meal, Boaz instructed his harvesters to grant her the special privilege of being allowed to glean among the sheaves, even to the point of dropping some handful of the harvest for her to glean. He ordered them not to rebuke her, apparently for overstepping the boundaries of those who are permitted to glean at the margins of the field.

That evening, she gathered a bushel of barley which she brought to Naomi along with what was left over from her meal. She told Naomi about Boaz, and Naomi prayed that he will be blessed for his kindness to the living and the dead. Ruth explained that Boaz told her to join the young women and work only in his field. To avoid having Ruth abused in someone else's field, Naomi advised Ruth to heed Boaz's words. Ruth continued to glean with the young women until the end of the barley and wheat harvests, which was approximately four months.

Lectio Divina

Spend 8 to 10 minutes in silent contemplation of the following passage:

The story of Ruth is a story of love and dedication. Ruth and Naomi had to endure difficulties, but they remained faithful to each other and to the Lord, and as a result, the Lord rewarded them with food and the protection of Boaz. The story offers a lesson about trusting God. No one escapes difficulties, but Jesus promised to be with us in our difficulties. He said, "Do not let your hearts be troubled. You have faith in God; have faith also in me" (John 14:1). Trust is a difficult virtue when all seems to be going wrong, but the story of Ruth encourages us to trust the Lord, no matter what happens.

✠ *What can I learn from this passage?*

Day 4: Ruth Marries Boaz (Ruth 3—4)

Naomi accepted the role of a concerned parent when she declared that she should be seeking a home pleasing for Ruth, which means that she should find a husband for Ruth. Since Boaz was a relative through Ruth's marriage to Elimelech, it would be proper for Ruth to marry one who has become her kin, even though she herself was a Moabite.

Naomi told Ruth to bathe, anoint herself, put on her best clothing, and go to the place where Boaz was threshing the grain. After Boaz finished working, eating, and drinking, she is to go where he slept, uncover a place at his feet, and lie down there. Ruth did as Naomi directed her, and after Boaz slept for awhile, he awoke and was startled to find a woman lying at his feet.

Ruth identified herself and asked Boaz to spread the wing of his cloak over her. This was an acceptable way for a woman to ask for a man to marry her. Ruth referred again to Boaz as a redeemer, which means one who has the call to help a relative, but Boaz declared that she had another redeemer who was a closer relative than he and had the first right to marry her. Boaz accepted her by encouraging her to remain where she was, showing that he would be willing to act as her redeemer, that is, marry her, if the other redeemer does not.

In the morning, Boaz alerted her to rise before anyone would know she had come, lest they think that Boaz shared sexually with her. He filled her shawl with grain to take home to Naomi.

Since many of the towns of the era of Boaz protected themselves with a wall, cases were settled at the gate to the town during the day. Boaz chose ten elders to act as witnesses for that which was about to take place. He explained that Naomi was putting up for sale a parcel of land that belonged to their kinsman, Elimelech. He sought an answer from the other redeemer, saying that if he did not exercise his right to buy the land, he, Boaz, would do it. Boaz reminded him that in buying the land, he must also acquire all responsibility for Ruth the Moabite, the widow of Elimelech, to raise a family for the deceased on his estate. Knowing that marrying Ruth would also give her offspring the right to his property, the redeemer decided to abdicate his right to Boaz.

In Deuteronomy, the law teaches that if anyone abdicates his rights to bear a child by his sister–in-law, whose child would then be considered a son of the deceased husband, he shall remove his sandal and give it as witness to his refusal (see Deuteronomy 25:5–10). Although Deuteronomy speaks of the rejected sister-in-law as receiving the sandal and spitting in the face of her brother-in-law, the Book of Ruth makes no reference to this part of the agreement. The other redeemer took off his sandal and gave it to Boaz.

Then Boaz called on the elders to be witnesses to the decision that gave him the right to acquire Ruth as his wife in order to raise a family for her late husband on his estate so that her late husband's name may not perish. The elders and others agreed to act as witnesses and prayed that the Lord would bless the house of Boaz, as the Lord blessed the house of Rachel and Leah, the two wives of Jacob who were daughters of Leban and who built up the house of Israel between them. Jacob had other children to help build up the house of Leban from some slave girls of Rachel and Leah.

The elders pray that the house of Boaz will become like the house of Perez, the son of Tamar and Judah. Judah refused to honor the Levirate law with his daughter-in-law by not allowing her to marry his youngest son after his first three sons, who married her, all died. Tamar disguised herself as a prostitute and tricked Judah into having a child through her. The firstborn son's name was Perez (see Genesis 38). Boaz belonged to the family line of Judah.

Boaz took Ruth as his wife and she bore a son. The people praised the Lord for providing a redeemer, that is, the boy born of Ruth was now a redeemer. Naomi took the child and cradled him as a gesture of affection. They named the boy Obed, who became the father of Jesse, who was the father of David. In this way, the author showed that among David's ancestry was a Moabite who was not born an Israelite. In the genealogy of Jesus found in Matthew's Gospel, Ruth is named as one of Jesus' ancestors.

Lectio Divina

Spend 8 to 10 minutes in silent contemplation of the following passage:

In the midst of stories about God choosing the people of Israel as the people of God, the author tells of a Moabite woman who is an ancestor of Jesus. The story hints at the idea of universal salvation. God rewards Ruth for her faithfulness and dedication, and she had no idea that her descendants would include a king for Israel and the birth of a child who is God. In an earlier reflection, we were told about the ripple effect of sin, but we can find in this story and its universal outcome the ripple effect of love and trust in the Lord.

✠ *What can I learn from this passage?*

Review Questions

1. What does the story of the Levite sending twelve parts of his concubine's body to the Israelites indicate about the era in which they lived?

2. In the story of the Judges, why does the author keep adding the words: "In those days, when there was no king in Israel . . . ." (19:1)? Why would the people want a king?

3. What is so important about the Book of Ruth? Reflect on Ruth's journey as well as her lineage.

4. What does Ruth's statement that Naomi's God will be her God reveal about the era in which Ruth and Naomi lived?

The Book of First Samuel (I)

1 SAMUEL 1–15

When Samuel went to sleep in his place, the LORD came and stood there, calling out as before: Samuel, Samuel! Samuel answered, "Speak, for your servant is listening" (3:9b–10).

Opening Prayer (SEE PAGE 16)

Context

Part 1: 1 Samuel 1—3 Hannah gives birth to Samuel, whom she dedicates to the Lord. Eli, the priest, had two sons who were wicked and cheated the people and the Lord out of their offerings. Eli rebuked his sons, but they did not heed his words. The Lord calls Samuel while he is sleeping and tells him that Eli's family is to be punished. Also, Samuel is acknowledged as a prophet.

Part 2: 1 Samuel 4—15 The Israelites lose the ark in a battle with the Philistines, and it is placed in the temple of a false god named Dagon, but the statue of Dagon is found face down in front of the ark. The Philistines return the ark to the Israelites. Samuel acts as a prophet and judge, calling the Israelites to repent and become faithful to the covenant. The Israelites want a king, and Saul is anointed as king. When Saul sins, Samuel announces that the Lord has rejected Saul.

PART 1: GROUP STUDY (1 SAMUEL 1—3)

Read aloud 1 Samuel 1—3.

1—2:11 Hannah Is Blessed With a Son

A man from Ephraim, named Elkanah, went yearly to Shiloh to offer sacrifice. Shiloh had become the central place of worship for the Israelites. The Ark of the Covenant was housed in a sanctuary (tabernacle) at Shiloh. The ark was a small wooden chest with angels standing on top with a space between them serving as a footstool for the Lord. The Israelites were forbidden to make an image of the one true God, so they made a footstool for the Lord who could not be seen. The ark contained the Ten Commandments.

The sanctuary consisted of a colorful tent with two rooms separated by a veil. The Ark of the Covenant was in the innermost section of the sanctuary while a gold lamp stand, table, and an altar for incense was in the outer room. A large courtyard for the people surrounded the sanctuary. Only the priests, who were descendants of Aaron, could enter the sanctuary and offer sacrifice. There were many lesser shrines throughout the Promised Land, but people visited the shrine at Shiloh as the central shrine because it housed the Ark of the Covenant.

Elkanah had two wives, the first named Hannah, who was barren, and the second named Peninnah, the mother of several children. Hannah suffered ridicule from Peninnah because of Hannah's inability to have children. Being barren was considered a curse to the Israelites since a family's name continued through their children. Elkanah, wishing to keep his posterity alive, may have married Peninnah when he realized that Hannah was not able to bear children.

As happened to many women in the Bible, Hannah's barrenness would turn to triumph as she bore a son named Samuel who would greatly affect the history of Israel. The Bible names other women who were considered barren until they bore significant sons for salvation history, women such as Sarah, who bore Isaac (Genesis 17:15–19); Rebekah, who bore Jacob (Genesis 25:21–22); and Elizabeth, who bore John the Baptist (Luke 1:8–24). When Hannah became depressed over her situation, Elkanah asked her why she felt despondent. Was not his love for her worth more than ten sons?

At one time, when Elkanah and his family went to Shiloh to worship, Eli the high priest saw Hannah weeping and praying in a manner that made him think she was drunk. In her prayer, she promised that if the Lord gave her a child, she would dedicate the child to the Lord. She added that no razor shall touch his head. The promise that no razor shall touch his head is part of the nazirite vow that requires abstaining from strong drink and not coming near the corpse of a dead person, including the corpses of their own parents (Numbers 6:1–21). Eli watched her lips moving, but she was praying silently, not out loud as was the custom.

When Eli confronted Hannah about her drunken appearance, she explained her situation, and Eli told her to go in peace, praying that the Lord would grant her prayer. Hannah took this as an affirmation that she would give birth to a child, and she went home and drank with her husband, a sign that her depressed state had ended. After their return home, Hannah became pregnant.

Hannah gave birth to Samuel and kept him until he was weaned, which could mean until he was three to six years old. She then took him to Eli, explained that she was the woman who prayed in his presence for a child, and that God granted her request. She added that she now dedicates the child to the Lord for as long as the child lives.

Hannah then proclaimed a prayer that sounded very much like Mary's "Magnificat," which is found in the Gospel of Luke when Mary visits her cousin (see Luke 1:46–55). The prayer was apparently a thanksgiving hymn written after the time of Hannah. The author inserted it here since it so closely reflects the sentiments of Hannah. It may have been used often by Israel in gratitude to God.

Hannah rejoiced in the Lord and declared that she drew her strength from God and can mock her enemies because of her victory. Keeping in mind that Peninnah ridiculed Hannah, the prayer fits the occasion since she now has victoriously given birth to a son. Hannah prays that the Lord is the creator of all and the guardian of all who can punish those who are evil. No one is able to contend with the Lord. The prayer ends with a plea for the Lord, the most high, to give strength to a king. This last blessing is in anticipation of the choice of a king, which will take place during Samuel's lifetime.

As the father of the child, Elkanah had the right to decide the fate of Samuel, but he earlier told Hannah to do with the child as she wished. He followed her wishes and left Samuel in Eli's service.

2:12–36 Wickedness of Eli's Sons

At the beginning of the book, the author tells us that the sons of Eli were ministering as priests of the Lord at Shiloh when Elkanah went to worship with his two wives. In the days of Eli, people worshiped at Shiloh, possibly in a large meeting tent, since Jerusalem was not yet the capital and the building of the temple was far off in the future.

When people made an offering, the priests were allowed to dip a fork in the boiling water and keep whatever they could bring up. Under the direction of Eli's sons, the priest's servants would use a three-pronged fork that would bring up more than an ordinary fork would carry. According to the Book of Leviticus, the fat of the offering belonged to the Lord and was to be burned (see Leviticus 7:22–27), but the servants of the sons of Eli would demand that the people give the raw meat to the priests, threatening those who refused to relinquish the raw meat. This was akin to stealing from the Lord.

Samuel would wear a linen ephod (a ceremonial apron worn by the priests) while serving in the Lord's presence. Hannah would bring some homemade garments for him when she came with her husband to worship and make the usual offering. God's favor was shown to Hannah as she bore three more sons and two daughters.

A man of God (a prophet) came to Eli with a message of doom for Eli and his family. The man of God, speaking in the name of God, recounted all that the Lord had done for the family of Eli from the time they were slaves in Egypt. The oracle of the messenger castigated Eli for choosing to honor his sons more than honoring the Lord. The day was coming when the house of Eli will come to an end. Eli did not stop his sons from sinning, although he did rebuke them for their actions. The prediction was that both of Eli's sons would die on the same day and be replaced by a faithful priest who shall do all that the Lord wished.

3:1–21 Samuel Acknowledged as a Prophet

One day, when Samuel was serving as a minister of the Lord under the direction of Eli and sleeping inside the Temple near the place where the ark was kept, he heard a voice calling him. Eli had grown old at this time, and his eyes had become so weak that he could hardly see. Samuel heard the voice four times. The first three times, he arose and went to Eli to learn what Eli wanted, and each time he had to awaken Eli. Finally, Eli realized that the Lord was calling Samuel, and he directed Samuel to answer, "Speak, for your servant is listening" (3:10). The fourth time the Lord called Samuel, he spoke these words and the Lord spoke to him. Samuel referred to himself here as a servant of the Lord.

The Lord predicted that Eli's family was about to experience a disaster. In a previous passage, the Lord warned Eli to reprove his sons because they were blaspheming the Lord by their actions, but Eli never did as the Lord commanded. Eli's sons still offered sacrifices to the Lord, but their offerings were not enough to compensate for their sins. Samuel feared passing the Lord's dreadful news on to Eli, but Eli threatened to curse Samuel if he refused to share the message of the Lord with him. Samuel informed Eli about the Lord's judgment, and Eli accepted the Lord's decision with resignation, knowing that the Lord will do what the Lord says.

Samuel became known as a trustworthy prophet of the Lord. A long time had passed since the Lord sent a prophet to Israel. After the Lord appeared and spoke to Samuel at Shiloh, Samuel spread God's word throughout Israel.

Review Questions

1. Why does the author of 1 Samuel stress the barrenness of Hannah?
2. What sin did the sons of Eli commit?
3. Why was Samuel so slow in realizing that it was the Lord who was calling him from sleep? In what ways have you heard the call of God?
4. Discuss and explain the significance of Samuel's call to be a prophet.

Closing Prayer (SEE PAGE 16)

Pray the closing prayer now or after *lectio divina*.

Lectio Divina (SEE PAGE 9)

Relax your body and maintain a posture of prayer (back straight, eyes shut, feet flat on the floor). This exercise can take as long as you want, but in the context of this Bible study, 10 to 20 minutes should be sufficient.

The meditations that follow are provided only to help group participants use this prayer form, but note that *lectio* is intended to bring one to a place of prayerful contemplation where the Word of God speaks to the hearer from his or her heart. (See page 9 for further instruction.)

Hannah's Prayer for a Son (1—2:11)

Hannah's prayer resembles the prayer of Mary, the mother of Jesus, when she visited Elizabeth. Both Hannah and Mary realize that they are servants of the Lord, and whatever part they play in God's plan of creation comes from the glory of the Lord and not from their own glory. Both were women of prayer, but they never saw themselves as worthy of any rewards from the Lord. The lesson is that whatever good we do in life comes from God, and, along with Mary and Hannah, we should always proclaim that it is the greatness of the Lord and not our own greatness that is evident through our good deeds and prayers.

✠ *What can I learn from this passage?*

Wickedness of Eli's Sons (2:12–36)

The sons of Eli held an important position in the land of Israel. The people depended on them to offer their sacrifices to the Lord. As ministers of the Lord, they sinned gravely in forcing the people to go against the Law of Moses. Jesus, speaking to those chosen to be his ministers, warns them: "Whoever causes one of these little ones who believe in me to sin, it would be better for him to have a great millstone hung around his neck and to be drowned in the depths of the sea" (Matthew 18:6). The condemnation of the sons of Eli and Jesus' warning for his ministers should inspire all Christians to fulfill their mission worthily and faithfully.

✠ *What can I learn from this passage?*

Samuel Acknowledged as a Prophet (3:1–21)

Samuel's response to the Lord should be heard from all Christians. It is a form of prayer that proclaims, "Speak, for your servant is listening" (3:10). Like Samuel, it may take several calls from the Lord before we are able to discern what the Lord asks of us, but in our prayer, reflections, and (if possible) with the help of a spiritual director, we may soon learn what the Lord is asking of us.

✠ *What can I learn from this passage?*

PART 2: INDIVIDUAL STUDY (1 SAMUEL 4—15)

Day 1: Battle With the Philistines (4—5)

The author digresses from the story of Samuel to speak about events surrounding the Ark of the Covenant. In a battle with the Philistines, the Israelites suffered such a great defeat and loss of life that they wondered why the Lord had abandoned them. As a result of the loss, the Israelites sent to Shiloh for the ark. The sons of Eli escorted the ark. When the Israelites saw it, they erupted into such a deafening clamor of joy that the Philistines became frightened. These Philistines did not believe in one god but in many gods, and they believed that the gods of the Israelites caused the plagues that killed the Egyptians in the wilderness. The leaders of the Philistines, however, rallied them, and they battled the Israelites, capturing the ark and killing the sons of Eli.

One of the men in the battle fled to Shiloh with the news that the sons of Eli were killed and that the Philistines had captured the ark. When Eli, who was now ninety-eight years old, heard the news of the catastrophe, especially the capture of the ark, he fell over backwards in his chair and broke his neck. Eli judged Israel for forty years, a number that signifies that he was judge for an entire generation.

The wife of Phinehas, who was present at the time, gave birth to a son when she learned that her husband was killed and that the Philistines captured the ark. She named the child Ichabod, which refers to the idea that glory has gone from Israel.

In ancient times, the people viewed combat as a battle between the gods. Those who won the battle proved that their gods were stronger. When the Philistines captured the ark, they believed that their god had proved to be more powerful and that they had captured the god of Israel. They brought the ark to Ashdod, one of five cities belonging to the Philistines. There they housed the ark in the temple of Dagon, a Canaanite god the Philistines chose as their most important god. They placed the ark next to the statue of Dagon. The Philistia consisted of five cities, each with its own king and temple.

The next morning, the Philistines found the statue of Dagon face down in front of the ark, as though worshiping the ark. They placed the statue of Dagon in its place, and again on the next morning found the statue face down in front of the ark. They placed it next to the ark. On the third morning, the trunk of the statue was lying face down, but the hands and head were smashed on the threshold of the Temple. In battle, when an army won the battle, they would cut off the hands and head of those taken captive. The God of the Israelites had conquered the god of the city of Ashdod.

The Lord afflicted the people of Ashdod to the point that they begged the Philistine leaders to remove the ark. The Philistines brought the ark to cities named Gath and Ekron, but in each place the people suffered dreadfully when the ark was in their vicinity. Tumors afflicted those who remained alive in these towns.

Lectio Divina

Spend 8 to 10 minutes in silent contemplation of the following passage:

A challenge for the people of ancient times was believing in the one true God, since they believed in several gods. When the Philistines turned against the one true God, they were punished and had to return the ark to the Israelites. In the world today, there are many challenges to the worship of the one true God. Some wish to completely erase any image of the true God from the public sector. Many atheistic governments have brought pain and suffering to their people. Christians have the task of proving that the one true God is more powerful than all the false gods of greed, vengeance, pleasure, or power.

✠ *What can I learn from this passage?*

Day 2: The Ark Returned (6—7)

After seven months, the priests and diviners of the people announced that if the Israelites wanted to return the ark to the Israelites, they would have to include an offering of five golden tumors and five golden mice with the ark. The priests added to the urgency of their announcement by reminding the leaders of the stubbornness of Egypt's Pharaoh and the tragedies the Egyptians had to endure before the Pharaoh allowed them to leave.

The priests directed the people to construct a cart and hitch two milk cows that have not borne a yoke. Their calves are forced inside, away from the cows that bore them. The cows that had given birth would not ordinarily leave their calves, which were shut up indoors. As a test of the power of God, they were to release two cows with the wagon, and if the cows went to Beth-shemesh, an Israelite city between Philistine and Israelite territory, then it was the Lord who brought this great catastrophe. If they did not go in this direction, all would know that it was not the Israelites' Lord but a bad streak of luck.

The two cows who had not borne a yoke would ordinarily amble back and forth since they were not trained to bear a yoke. Because they were milk cows bearing a yoke for the first time, they would serve as a pure offering to the Lord of Israel if they went in the direction of the Israelites. Proving that the Lord wished the ark to go to the Israelites, the cows immediately headed toward Beth-shemesh in front of the five leaders who followed them to the borders of the area. The author notes that the cows were mooing as they dragged the ark, emphasizing their desire to feed their young calves.

The cart stopped at a large stone in an area known as the field of Joshua. The Israelites, who were harvesting grain, rejoiced when they saw the ark returned. They cut up the cart, started a fire with the wood, and offered the cows as a burnt offering to the Lord. The Levites, who alone were permitted to touch the ark, placed the ark and the box with the golden articles on the stone. The five golden tumors represented the leaders and the five golden mice the five cities of the Philistines.

The people celebrated with joy, but seventy men, who refused to celebrate, died because they did not join in the celebration. The people, shocked and saddened by these deaths, sent for someone who could "stand in the presence of the LORD" (6:20), which refers to someone engaged in priestly service. Levites who were neither priests nor descendants of the Levite Aaron were present to move the Ark of the Covenant. Abinadab appointed his son, Eleazar, as the guardian of the ark. The identity of Abinadab is not clear in this passage.

As the Philistines prepared to attack the Israelites at Mizpah, the terrified Israelites petitioned Samuel to pray to the Lord for them. Samuel, crying out for help, offered an unweaned whole lamb to the Lord as a burnt offering. In so doing, he performed the role of priest and followed in the footsteps of Moses, who interceded for the people during their sojourn in the desert. Claps of thunder, which the people believed was the voice of the Lord, bewildered the Philistines, and the Israelites overpowered them. They named the place "Ebenezer," which means "stone of the helper," a reference to the Lord.

Lectio Divina

Spend 8 to 10 minutes in silent contemplation of the following passage:

> When the ark was returned, the people rejoiced because they saw it as the return of the God of Israel in their presence. In the Gospels, we learn that God is with us always when Matthew writes "'they shall name him Emmanuel,' which means 'God is with us'" (Matthew 1:23). The emphasis on God's presence is repeated at the end of Matthew's Gospel when Jesus proclaims, "I am with you always, until the end of the age" (Matthew 28:20). God's presence in their midst was as important to the Israelites as Christ's continual presence is among us.

✠ *What can I learn from this passage?*

Day 3: Request for a King (8—9)

Samuel had two sons who, like the sons of Eli, did not follow the lead of their father but sought to enrich themselves by accepting bribes and acting unjustly. When the people saw this, they asked Samuel to appoint a king over them similar to the kings in the nations around them. In this passage, the idea of appointing a king was greeted by Samuel with displeasure.

When Samuel appealed to the Lord, he learned that the people were not rejecting Samuel, but they were rejecting the Lord, who is the true king of Israel. The Lord directed Samuel to listen to the people and to warn them of the rights of the king who will rule them.

Samuel warned of the dire outcome of having a king. He told the people that the king will assign their sons to chariots for battle, appoint commanders from among them, make them work in his fields and produce his weapons, use their daughters to serve his household needs, confiscate their fields and groves for his servants, tithe their crops, take their slaves and animals to do his work, tithe their flocks, and make slaves of them. The prophet Samuel emphasized that this would happen to such an extent that they will eventually cry out to the Lord for help, but the Lord will not listen to them. From a later point in history, possibly during the reign of Solomon, the author wrote these warnings.

After hearing Samuel's warnings, the people still clamored for a king, so the Lord told Samuel to listen to them and appoint a king to rule them. Samuel directed the people to return home while he searched for a king.

A man named Saul, who was destined to be king, is described in the usual fashion of heroes in the Bible, handsome, young, and head and shoulders above all the people. Two donkeys of Saul's father, Kish, wandered off, and Kish sent Saul and one of the servants to find the donkeys. After a long search, Saul said to the servant that they should return to his father, lest his father become more concerned about him than the donkeys. The servant said that a man of God, who was held in high esteem, was in the city.

The day before, the Lord revealed to Samuel that he would meet a man from the land of Benjamin whom he was to anoint as ruler of the people. When Samuel saw Saul, the Lord told Samuel that this was the man who will lead Israel. Saul asked Samuel where the seer was, and Samuel identifies himself as the seer. Samuel sat Saul and his servant at the head of the table with approximately thirty guests. He ordered the cook to place the reserved portion before Saul, saying that it was kept for him. Saul dined with Samuel, and when they came down from the high place, a mattress was spread for Saul on the roof.

Lectio Divina

Spend 8 to 10 minutes in silent contemplation of the following passage:

According to the Scriptures, the Lord chose Saul as the first king of Israel. When Jesus is speaking to his disciples, he tells them, "It was not you who chose me, but I who chose you and appointed you to go and bear fruit that will remain" (John 15:16). The Lord has a plan and chooses each one of us to fulfill that plan. God does not force us to accept God's choice in our lives, but God invites us and we are free to respond. God's choice for us is not always clear, and we must struggle to discern the Lord's choice. It can seem menial or great, but in God's eye, every choice is important.

✠ *What can I learn from this passage?*

Day 4: Saul Chosen King (10—12)

Samuel took a flask of oil and poured it over Saul's head and kissed him, saying that the Lord anoints him as ruler over his people, that he will govern his people and save them from the power of the enemy all around them. Samuel predicted that Saul would meet two men near Rachel's tomb, in the territory of Benjamin, who will tell him that the donkeys have been found and that his father is anxious about him. After that, three men will meet them as they go up to God at Bethel. One will be bringing three young goats, another three loaves of bread, and a third a skin of wine. When they greet them, the men will offer them two offerings of bread, which Saul is instructed to accept.

After that, he will enter the Philistine garrison where he will meet a band of prophets coming from the high place, preceded by lyres, tambourines, flutes, and harps, and in a prophetic ecstasy. Samuel predicts that the spirit of the Lord will rush upon Saul, and he will join in their prophetic ecstasy, and will become a changed man. He tells them to go ahead of him to Gilgal, where Samuel will come to him to offer burnt offerings and to sacrifice communion offerings. Samuel tells him to wait seven days until he returns. Then Samuel will tell Saul what he must do. All the signs promised were fulfilled that day.

Samuel gathered the people before the Lord at Mizpah and addressed them, beginning with the history of the Israelites as they brought Israel up from Egypt and delivered them from the power of the Egyptians and all the people who oppressed them. Samuel had them stand before the Lord according to their tribes and families. The tribe of Benjamin, the clan of Matri, and finally, Saul, the son of Kish, were all chosen. Saul stood head and shoulders over all. Samuel asks the people if they see the man chosen by the Lord, stating that there is no one like him among all the people. The people, recognizing Saul, shouted, "Long live the king!"

Samuel explained to the people about the rules of the monarchy, wrote them in a book, and placed them before the presence of the Lord. Samuel sent all the people home and returned home himself, accompanied by warriors whose hearts the Lord had touched. Some rejected Saul, asking how this person can save them. They despised him and brought him no tribute.

Nahash, the Ammonite, besieged Jabesh, and people begged for a treaty, but Nahash said the treaty would consist in gouging out their right eyes. The elders of the people of Jabesh asked for seven days to send out among the Israelites to discover if anyone would save them. If not, they would surrender. The messengers arrived at Gibeah of Saul. When Saul came in from the field and saw the people weeping, he learned about the plight of Jabesh and, in his anger, the spirit of the Lord came upon him. He cut his yoke of oxen into pieces and sent them throughout the territory of the Israelites, warning that those who do not follow him and Samuel will have the same done to all their oxen. The scene recalls an earlier scene when a Levite cuts up his concubine, sending a piece to each of the tribes to rally them to fight.

The people feared the Lord and joined Saul and Samuel. Saul sent messengers to the people of Jabesh, saying they would be rescued the following day. The people told Nahash that they would surrender the following day and he may do whatever he wished with them. On the following dawn, however, Saul arranged his troops into three companies and invaded the Ammonite camp, killing them as the day became hotter. The Ammonites scattered to the point that no two accompanied each other.

When the people saw this, they wanted Saul to kill those who previously refused to follow Saul as their leader, but Saul objected, saying that the Lord rescued Israel on that day, which meant that it was not time for him to shed Israelite blood. All the people then went to Gilgal where, in the Lord's presence, they made Saul king. They sacrificed a communion offering before the Lord, and Saul and the Israelites celebrated.

In a transition from leadership by a judge to leadership by a king, Samuel addresses the people, contrasting his leadership with the dire warnings that he described concerning the leadership of a king found in an earlier chapter of the Bible where he described how the king will force them and their possessions to serve him (8:10–22). Although he has served them from his youth, he declares that he has now grown old and gray, and they can verify this since they are familiar with his sons who are adults. Samuel asked the people to name anyone from whom he has taken an ox or a donkey, or anyone he has cheated or wronged. The people responded that Samuel has not taken advantage of them in any manner.

Samuel recalled how the Lord cared for the people in the time of Moses and Aaron, and how the Israelites abandoned the Lord. Despite the support the Lord gave through the leadership of the judges, the people asked Samuel for a king to lead them when Nahash threatened them. In this passage, their call for a king is seen as a rejection of the Lord as their king.

Samuel informs the people that the Lord will bless them as long as they and the king are faithful to the Lord, and that the Lord will abandon them if they are unfaithful. At the harvest time of year, the people know that there is little or no rain, so Samuel offers a miracle as a sign supporting his words, calling upon the Lord to send thunder and rain on them, which the Lord does. He is emphasizing the extent of their sin in asking for a king.

The frightened people beg Samuel to pray that the Lord will overlook this new evil in seeking a king. Samuel agrees that they have committed evil, but as long as they serve the Lord with their whole heart and do not turn to other gods who do not exist, the Lord will remain with them.

Lectio Divina

Spend 8 to 10 minutes in silent contemplation of the following passage:

Although God chooses each one of us to fulfill a certain role in life and that choice is important to God's plan, we are still free to accept it, reject it, or act against it. Saul must remain faithful to the covenant or the Lord will take the kingly line away from his offspring and choose another. No matter what God calls us to do, we must remain faithful to God in fulfilling our call.

✠ *What can I learn from this passage?*

Day 5: Rejection of Saul (13—15)

Samuel told Saul to wait seven days for him to come to Saul before moving. When Samuel did not appear, some members of his army became impatient and abandoned Saul. In light of the diminishing number of combatants in his army, Saul apparently became nervous and as impatient as his army. He decided not to wait for Samuel but to sacrifice the burnt offering and communion offering himself.

When Saul finished sacrificing his offering, Samuel arrived and demanded to know what Saul had done. Saul tells Samuel that he offered a sacrifice because some members of the army abandoned him, and he had not sought the Lord's blessing. He knew that the Philistines would be coming down to attack him. Samuel informed Saul that if he had kept the Lord's command, the Lord would have established his kingship in Israel forever, but since he did not keep the Lord's command, his kingship would not endure, that is, his offspring would not become kings.

Samuel informed Saul that the Lord sought out a man after the Lord's own heart, which was a reference to David, who will succeed Saul as king. The phrase, "a man after the Lord's own heart," meant someone chosen by the Lord.

One day, Jonathan, depending on the strength of the Lord to be with him, went with his armor-bearer to the Philistine outpost without telling his father. When the Philistines saw Jonathan and his armor-bearer, they told them to come up so they could teach them a lesson. On that day, when Jonathan and his armor-bearer killed about twenty men, terror spread throughout the Philistine camp. Saul, who saw that the enemy was scattered and running in all directions, ordered those around him to find out if any of the troops were missing. They found that Jonathan and his armor-bearer were missing. Saul, realizing that the Philistines were running around confused and even killing each other, went into the battle and forced the Philistines to flee.

As the battle continued, Saul put a curse on any man who would eat before he could avenge himself of his enemies. They saw a honeycomb on the ground but did not eat of its honey. Jonathan, however, unaware that his father had put the army under an oath not to eat, took some honey from the cone, and it energized him. When one of the soldiers saw this, he informed Jonathan about his father's strict oath. Jonathan expressed his disagreement with his father's foolish command, saying that the slaughter of the Philistines would be greater if his father allowed the men to eat of the plunder. If they ate, they would have more energy for the battle.

When the Israelites defeated a segment of the Philistine army, Saul's exhausted and hungry combatants slaughter the sheep, oxen, and calves without draining the blood from them and eat the meat with the blood in it. This was a serious violation of the Lord's command to the Israelites, forbidding them to eat meat with blood in it (see Leviticus 19:26). When Saul heard of the sin of his army, he had his men bring the plunder to him and, rolling a large stone in front of him, he ordered them to slaughter the animals in his presence and eat the meat without the blood in it. Slaughtering the animals on the stone would allow the blood to flow from the animals before they were declared drained of the blood.

As Saul prepared for another battle against the Philistines, he consulted a priest to determine if the Lord would deliver the enemy into his hands, but he received no answer from the Lord, a sign that someone in his army had committed an offense against the Lord. Saul had the army stand on one side while he and Jonathan stood on the other. The Lord pointed out Jonathan as the offender, and Jonathan admitted that he had taken some honey, despite the oath his father took before the battle that no one shall eat until the Philistines were defeated. Jonathan, however, was not aware of his father's oath when he ate the honey. He asks in desperation if he is to die for taking a little honey on his staff.

Saul reluctantly remained adamant, refusing to free Jonathan from death, which would be the result of the foolish oath Saul made to the Lord. When the army objected, supporting Jonathan—who had won a great victory against the Philistines—Jonathan's life was spared. Samuel reported to Saul that the Lord was about to punish the tribe of Amalek for all they did against the Israelites as they journeyed from Egypt to the Promised Land. According to the Book of Deuteronomy, the tribe of Amalek struck at the rear of the Israelites during their journey in the desert, hindering their passage and killing many (see Deuteronomy 25:17–19). Saul warned a tribe known as the Kenites to leave the tribe of Amalek so that they would not be obliterated like the tribe of Amalek. Saul and his army slaughtered the inhabitants of Amalek, with the exception of Agag, king of Amalek, and the best of their livestock.

As a result of Saul's sparing of Agag and some of the livestock, the Lord regretted making Saul a king. When Samuel received this word from the Lord, he became enraged and prayed all night before going to meet with Saul. Saul, in the meanwhile, became proud of his victories. When Samuel finally met with Saul, Saul protested that he had followed all the Lord's commands. Samuel asked with a tone of disdain what the noise of bleating of sheep and lowing of oxen meant.

Saul sought to exonerate himself by saying that he kept the best animals for a sacrificial offering to the Lord, but Samuel informed him that the Lord commanded him to completely destroy all the Amalekites and their livestock. Samuel asked whether the Lord delights more in burnt offerings and sacrifices as much as obedience, which is better than sacrifices. In disobeying the Lord, Saul committed a sin of pride, which is akin to idolatry. Because Saul rejected the Lord's command, the Lord rejected him.

As Samuel turned to leave, Saul seized an end of his garment, which is a way of pleading with the one offended. When the end of Samuel's garment tore away, Samuel used the occasion to predict that the Lord has torn the kingdom of Israel from Saul and that it has been given to a neighbor who was better than Saul. This is the second story about the Lord's rejection of Saul. This could indicate that these two stories come from two separate authors.

When Saul begged Samuel to go with him to offer sacrifice, Samuel reluctantly agreed. After worshiping, Samuel demanded that Agag, the king of Amalek, be brought to him, stating that just as Amalek's sword has made many women childless, so now will Samuel make Amalek's mother childless. Samuel killed Agag and left, never again to meet with Saul.

Lectio Divina

Spend 8 to 10 minutes in silent contemplation of the following passage:

Because Saul sinned, his descendants will not reign as king of Israel. Saul's life is an example of a good person becoming evil over time. Living a life pleasing to the Lord is a daily challenge. We can never say that we are perfect and that we will never sin. Holy people pray each day that God will keep them from sin that day.

✠ *What can I learn from this passage?*

Review Questions

1. Why did possessing the Ark of the Covenant cause problems for the Philistines?
2. Why did the Israelites want a king?
3. What sin did Saul commit by offering sacrifice in the place of Samuel?
4. How would the Lord, who knows all, feel any regrets as the Lord did in making Saul a king?

The Book of First Samuel (II)

1 SAMUEL 16—31

Then Samuel, with the horn of oil in hand, anointed him in the midst of his brothers, and from that day on, the spirit of the LORD rushed upon David (16:13).

Opening Prayer (SEE PAGE 16)

Context

Part 1: 1 Samuel 16—18 Samuel goes to Bethlehem, where he anoints David king. David kills Goliath, making Saul take notice of him. David and Jonathan become close friends. Saul becomes jealous of David's successes and plots to kill him.

Part 2: 1 Samuel 19—31 David and Jonathan enter into an agreement that David will not harm Jonathan's offspring if Jonathan should die. David learns that Saul is seeking his life, and he leads his men away from Saul. Saul has the priests killed because they gave bread to David. David has opportunities to kill Saul, but he refuses to raise his hand against the Lord's anointed. Saul and Jonathan are killed in battle.

PART 1: GROUP STUDY (1 SAMUEL 16—18)

Read aloud 1 Samuel 16—18.

16:1–23 Samuel Anoints David

Samuel had placed his hopes in Saul as a worthy king of the people, but Saul abandoned the Lord who now rejected him. The Lord directed Samuel to go to Bethlehem with a heifer, appearing to travel there to sacrifice the heifer to the Lord. He was to invite Jesse and his sons to the sacrifice and anoint the son that the Lord pointed out to him. Samuel did as the Lord said, inviting Jesse with his sons to the feast, expecting that the Lord would point out the one to be anointed king. Jesse presented his oldest son, Eliab, to Samuel. Eliab fit all the external images worthy of a king. He had a lofty stature like Saul, but the Lord tells Samuel not to judge by external appearances.

The story reads like a modern fairy tale. After Jesse presented seven sons whom the Lord rejected, Samuel asked if Jesse had any more sons. When Jesse said that he had another son who was tending the sheep, Samuel ordered Jesse to send for him. David was presented as a shepherd, a common image used to designate a king. David arrived with the usual majestic looks that accompany one chosen by the Lord. He was young, ruddy, good-looking, and had beautiful eyes. The Lord chose David and ordered Samuel to anoint him. When Samuel anointed David, the spirit of the Lord rushed upon him.

The author of 2 Samuel will speak of David being anointed as king two more times after Saul dies, events that give evidence that the story of the anointing of David as king comes from more than one author. In the chapters ahead, the same evidence of several sources will appear again when the author speaks of Saul's relationship with David. Further evidence of multiple sources comes from an event in the next chapter, when Eliab, one of David's brothers, seemed unaware of David being anointed, although this passage spoke of David being anointed in the midst of his brothers.

In contrast to David's reception of the spirit of the Lord, the spirit departed from Saul, leaving him tormented by an evil spirit, which could be a reference to some mental disorder afflicting Saul. The text subtly speaks of Saul's evil spirit as coming from God, perhaps to stress that the Lord had totally abandoned Saul. The servants requested permission to have a harpist present to play music for Saul when the evil spirits tormented him. One of the servants told him about a son of Jesse of Bethlehem who was a skilled harpist, a brave warrior, an able speaker, and a handsome young man, all of which is an idealistic picture of someone suited to be king.

At Saul's request, Jesse sent David to Saul with a customary offering which, in this case, were five loaves of bread, a skin of wine, and a goat. Whenever the Lord sent the evil spirit on Saul, David would soothe him with his harp and the evil spirit would leave Saul.

Saul became so fond of David that he made him his armor-bearer, a sign that identified him as a warrior and a trusted servant of Saul.

17:1–54 David and Goliath

Goliath was a champion of the Philistines. The author says that Goliath was nine and a half feet tall, which was most likely an idealized image of Goliath as a giant. He had a bronze helmet and a bronze breastplate weighing a little more than 125 pounds, armor reaching from the ankle to the knee, and a bronze sword slung from his shoulder. His javelin had an iron head weighing more than fifteen pounds. The weight and form of his weapons showed Goliath to be as strong as he was tall. His shield-bearer went ahead of him. Goliath challenged the Israelites to choose one of their men to fight him. If the Israelite killed Goliath, then the giant declared that the Philistines will be vassals of the Israelites, but if Goliath killed the champion of the Israelites, then the opposite would be true. His words terrified Saul and the Israelites.

David went to the battle line, where he met his brothers, who were in Saul's army, and heard Goliath taunt the Israelites. The terrified Israelites testified that the king would make whoever killed Goliath a very wealthy person. Saul would give him his daughter in marriage and exempt his father's family from paying taxes.

David arrogantly asked who this uncircumcised Philistine was that he should insult the armies of the living God. David's words were reported to Saul, who sent for David.

When David appeared before Saul, he asked to be allowed to fight Goliath, but Saul objected, stating that David was only a youth while Goliath had been a warrior since his youth. David defended his stance by saying he had to fight off lions and bears to protect sheep from these predators, seizing them by the throat and killing them. Saul told David to go, praying that the Lord would be with him.

When they dressed David in Saul's tunic, put a bronze helmet on his head, and a coat of armor around him, David objected that he could not battle with this armor since he was not used to it. He took off the armor, took his staff and five smooth stones in the pocket of his shepherd's bag, and approached the Philistine with his sling in hand.

The Philistine cursed David by the Philistine gods and declared that he would feed David's flesh to the birds and the beasts. David chided the giant, saying that Goliath came out after him well-armed, but David came out in the name of the God of the Israelites. David predicted that the Lord would deliver the Philistine into his hand. Because of the apparent mismatch between David and the giant, all people will realize that it is not the sword or spear that is powerful but the God of the Israelites.

As David and the Philistine ran to the battle line, David put a stone in his sling and hurled it at the Philistine, hitting him in the forehead and embedding it in his brow. When the giant toppled to the ground on his face, David struck the Philistine dead. Although the author already said that David struck the Philistine dead, he speaks again of David killing the giant, this time by killing him and then cutting off his head.

Upon the death of their hero, the Philistines fled and the Israelites pursued them, wounding and killing many of them. The author relates that the Israelites looted the camp of the Philistines and that David brought the head of Goliath to Jerusalem. It is unlikely that David would have brought the head to Jerusalem at this time, since Jerusalem was not an Israelite city but a Jebusite city. David would later capture Jerusalem and make it the center of Israel. Although the author stated that David kept Goliath's armor in his own tent, this is also unlikely, since David—who was not portrayed as a warrior in this passage—would not yet have a military tent.

17:55—18:30 David and Jonathan

Although an earlier tradition told us that David was brought to Saul to soothe Saul's evil moods, an editor draws from a different tradition to show Saul's acceptance of David as though he does not know Saul. In this tradition, Saul inquires from his general, Abner, about the identity of David's father. Abner replied that he did not know, so when David came into Saul's presence carrying the head, Saul asked David who his father is. David replied that he is the son of Jesse of Bethlehem.

According to the author, Jonathan, the son of Saul, loved David and bound himself in a loving friendship with him. In using the term "love," the author implies that Jonathan is politically loyal to David as well as having a special fondness for him. Jonathan handed over the cloak he was wearing to David, along with his military dress, his sword, bow, and belt. This implied that Jonathan was handing over the succession to the throne to David, a subtle message given by the author of this passage. David became so successful in battle that Saul set him over his soldiers, a gesture which gained the approval of the army, including its officers.

After one of David's victories over the Philistines, women met David, dancing, playing tambourines and harps, and singing, "Saul has slain his thousands, David his tens of thousands" (18:7). This ignited a strong emotion of jealousy in Saul, who now looked for an occasion to kill David. Twice, when David was playing the harp for Saul, Saul threw his spear at David with the intent of pinning David to the wall, but each time David escaped.

When Saul offered his daughter, Merob, to David in marriage, David objected, pointing to his humble origins and asking who is he that he should become the son-in-law of the king. This would make him a possible heir to the throne if Saul's sons died. Saul changed his mind and gave his daughter in marriage to another.

When Saul learned that his second daughter, Michal, loved David, he again announced to David that he would become his son-in-law. David, realizing that the father of the bride set the price that the future husband must pay and that he himself was poor, objected. Instead of asking for possessions from David, Saul asked for the foreskins of a hundred Philistines.

Saul's intent was to have David killed by the Philistines as he attempted to bring back the foreskins.

In David's era, it was not uncommon for victors to bring back some part of the enemies' bodies. David and his men killed 200 Philistines and brought their foreskins back to Saul, who had no choice but to give his daughter, Michal, to David as his wife. Saul, realizing that the Lord was with David and that his daughter loved David, became even more fearful of him.

Review Questions

1. How did Samuel choose David as king? Discuss the selection process.
2. Why did David believe that it was important for him to fight Goliath?
3. Was Saul correct in believing that he had to rid himself of David? Explain.

Closing Prayer (SEE PAGE 16)

Pray the closing prayer now or after *lectio divina*.

Lectio Divina (SEE PAGE 9)

Relax your body and maintain a posture of prayer (back straight, eyes shut, feet flat on the floor). This exercise can take as long as you want, but in the context of this Bible study, 10 to 20 minutes should be sufficient.

The meditations that follow are provided only to help group participants use this prayer form, but note that *lectio* is intended to bring one to a place of prayerful contemplation where the Word of God speaks to the hearer from his or her heart. (See page 9 for further instruction.)

Samuel Anoints David (16:1–23)

We all are called to a mission in life, but if we fail to fulfill our call, the Lord can choose someone else to fulfill God's plan. God chose Saul, but Saul failed, so the Lord chose David, who would become a great king in Israel. We are never sure what God's plan is for us, but through daily prayer and loving others, we show that we are attempting to fulfill God's plan in some manner.

✠ *What can I learn from this passage?*

David and Goliath (17:1–54)

When Jesus tells his disciples how difficult it is for a rich man to enter heaven, they ask who then could be saved. Jesus answered, "For human beings this is impossible, but for God all things are possible" (Matthew 19:26). Jesus' words apply not only to his message about wealth but to every aspect of life. David, who is too small to wear armor, kills a giant warrior. Impossible! But David had God on his side, and with God, all things are possible. This fact encourages Christians never to abandon doing good. When it seems that evil will conquer, Christians still have hope, because all things are possible for God.

 ✠ *What can I learn from this passage?*

David and Jonathan (17:55—18:30)

Jonathan and David had a loving friendship, one that allowed Jonathan to willingly accept that David would be king. Central to God's creation are friendship and love. Jesus had a loving friendship with the family of Martha, Mary, and Lazarus. In the Gospel of John, we read that Jesus "loved Martha and her sister and Lazarus" (John 11:5). Love is not something arbitrary in life; it is necessary for humans to love. When Jesus commanded us to love, he was speaking of loving all people, not just the people who are easy to love. Jesus told his disciples, "This I command you: love one another" (John 15:17). Love is very important in creation.

 ✠ *What can I learn from this passage?*

PART 2: INDIVIDUAL STUDY (1 SAMUEL 19—31)

Day 1: David's Flight (19—22)

When Saul discussed his intention to kill David with Jonathan and all his servants, Jonathan, who loved David, warned him to hide from the king until Jonathan had an opportunity to speak with him. Jonathan defended David before Saul. When Saul swore an oath that he would not kill David, Jonathan informed David about his discussion with his father, and he brought David back into the service of Saul.

After swearing not to kill David, Saul, irritated again by an evil spirit, threw his spear at David, intending to pin him to the wall, but David eluded the spear. Later that night, Saul sent guards to David's house with plans to kill him in the morning. Michal warned David that he must run for his life, and she let him down through a window. David's house, like many of the houses in the city, was apparently built against the city wall, which allowed David to flee from the city once he was lowered to the ground.

Once David left, Michal took the "teraphim," which was a life-sized image of a household god, laid it on the bed, put a tangle of goat hair at its head, and covered it with a blanket. When the officers came to take David, Michal said that he was in bed sick. Saul ordered his soldiers to bring David to him in his bed so that Saul could kill him. When they found the teraphim and not David in the bed, Saul asked his daughter why she lied. She said that David threatened to kill her if she would not let him go.

After David's escape, Saul learned that David was with Samuel at Ramah. When Saul sent his soldiers to capture David, he encountered a band of prophets, led by Samuel, who were in a prophetic state. The Spirit of the Lord came upon the soldiers and the prophetic state enveloped them. Saul sent messengers to Ramah two more times, but each time Saul's men fell into a prophetic state. Saul himself also went to Ramah and likewise fell into a prophetic state.

The author writes that Saul lost control of himself in the presence of Samuel, despite an earlier message that Samuel never again saw Saul (15:35). This passage is further evidence that the editor is gathering different sources together in his message. Saul stripped himself naked. He lay naked all day and all night, thus degrading himself and his role as king. Saul received from the Lord a place among the prophets, not for a blessing, but for the protection of David.

David did not know what he did that caused Saul's strong desire to kill him. David tells Jonathan that his father knew Jonathan's affection for him and that he has decided not to tell Jonathan what he intended to do. David plotted with Jonathan, telling him that the next day is the new moon, which is the day of sacrificing and feasting. If it happens that his father misses David, Jonathan was to tell him that David requested that he allow David to go and join his whole clan in its seasonal offering. And if Saul reacted by showing relief and saying that his servant is safe, then all is well. However, if Saul becomes angry, then it is clear that he has planned some harm for David. Jonathan promised to tell David if his father plans on harming him.

Jonathan swore an oath in the usual manner, saying, "may the Lord do thus to Jonathan and more" if he did not warn David. Jonathan believed David would become king. He made David promise that he will treat Jonathan well if he is still alive when the Lord is with David, as he was with his father at an earlier time. If Jonathan died, then David must treat his family well and never cut his name away from the family of David.

Jonathan told David that he will warn David if it is safe or not by shooting arrows as though he were shooting target practice. David was to hide nearby, and if Jonathan said to his attendant that if the arrow is on his side, it will be safe for David to come. But if he said to the attendant that the arrow is beyond him, then David was to leave, for the Lord was then sending him away.

When David was absent from the feast on the first day of the new moon, Saul thought that David became unclean by accident. There were a number of ways a person could become ritually unclean. On the second day, the king asked Jonathan about David, and Jonathan told his father that he gave David permission to go to his clan for the seasonal sacrifice.

Recognizing that Jonathan had excused David for another reason, Saul became enraged and insulted his son, calling him the son of a rebellious woman. Saul stated that Jonathan will not make good his claim to kingship as long as David lives, but Jonathan angrily asked why David should die. Saul wielded his spear to strike Jonathan, and Jonathan leaped from the table in a rage and ate nothing that day because of being grieved over David and being humiliated by his father.

Jonathan went out into the field with his attendant and shot the arrow farther out, telling his attendant that the arrow was beyond, a sign to David that all was not well. After recovering the arrows, Jonathan sent his attendant away and, after a tearful greeting, Jonathan bid David farewell, reminding him of his oath binding him to David and his offspring to David's offspring.

David became a fugitive and arrived before Ahimelech, a great grand-son of Eli the priest during the early life of Samuel. Ahimelech trembled before David, perhaps because he is aware that David is fleeing from the king. David, however, lied, telling Ahimelech that the king sent him on a special secret mission and that he will soon meet with some of Saul's men. He asked for five loaves of bread, but Ahimelech states that he only has holy bread. If the men David is meeting have abstained from women, then Ahimelech can give him the bread. David answered that they have abstained from women in preparation for the campaign, so Ahimelech gave the bread to David.

A man named Doeg, who was an Edomite and one of Saul's servants, was present and apparently detained before the Lord because he had a vow to fulfill. Since he was the chief of Saul's shepherds, he would have ready access to the king.

David, who feigned that he had to leave the king hastily for urgent business, asked the priest if he had any weapons for him. The priest stated that he had only the sword of Goliath, whom David had killed. The priest offered David the sword, and David took it.

Doeg, the Edmonite, told Saul that he saw the priest Ahimelech consult the Lord for David and give him the sword of Goliath. Ahimelech did give bread and Goliath's sword to David, but he did not consult the Lord for him. This, however, became an accusation which Ahimelech did not deny, becoming the center of this episode. He pointed out that this was not the first time he consulted the Lord for David. Ahimelech denied knowing anything about the situation at hand, knowing only that David was loyal to the king.

Saul commanded his soldiers to kill the priests of the Lord and their families, but the soldiers refused to strike the priests. Saul ordered Doeg to kill the priests, and Doeg, being an Edmonite, did not fear the priests' relationship to the Lord and killed eighty-five of them. Saul then slaugh-tered the people of the priestly city, including all the men, women, children, and livestock. Abiathar, a grandson of Ahimelech, escaped and reported to David all that happened. When the sons of Eli sinned, the Lord predicted that there would be one faithful priest left to the house of Eli; Abiathar was that sole surviving priest (see 1 Samuel 2:27–36).

Lectio Divina

Spend 8 to 10 minutes in silent contemplation of the following passage:

> Those who protect David risk being killed or rejected by Saul, yet
> they are still willing to protect him. Throughout history, people have
> risked their lives to protect another who is in danger. In some cases,
> those who protected others did not even know them before they
> helped them, such as the people who hid the Jews from the Nazi
> army. Jesus gave us a law of love, and love can demand risking our
> lives for the sake of others, even those we do not know.

✠ *What can I learn from this passage?*

Day 2: David Spares Saul (23—25)

When Saul was pursuing David, he went into a cave to relieve himself. David
and his men were deep within the cave. David's servants rejoiced, saying
that the Lord had delivered Saul into his hands. David snuck up quietly
and cut off the end of Saul's robe without Saul's knowing it. But he later
regretted his action, saying that he should not have done this to the Lord's
anointed. The men wanted David to kill Saul, but David refused. When Saul
left the cave, David shouted to him from the entrance to the cave that he
had an opportunity to kill Saul but could not do this to the Lord's anointed.
He held up the piece of cloth from Saul's robe to show that he had this
opportunity, and he called upon the Lord to judge between him and Saul.

Saul addressed David as his son and wept when he admitted that David treated him graciously. He admitted that the Lord delivered him into
David's hands and declared that he knew that David will certainly become
king. Samuel died, and a large number of Israelites gathered to mourn him,
burying him at Ramah.

David heard that a man named Nabal was shearing his sheep. Sheep-
shearing time was a time for festivities and generosity. David, whose army
protected the area, sent ten men to greet Nabal and seek gifts from him.
Nabal responded by belittling David, asking who he, the son of Jesse, is.
He asked if he should give his bread, wine, and meat to David and his men.
When David's men reported what Nabal said, David had them strap on
their swords and set out for battle with 400 men.

Abigail, Nabal's wife, learned of Nabal's refusal from her servants who spoke of the good David and his men provided for them. They told Abigail to do what she can to save the people. She quickly gathered a large offering of bread, wine, sheep, and other produce and loaded them on a donkey. She met David outside the city and paid homage to him as though he were already a king. She also pointed out that Nabal's name means "fool" and that he acts like a fool. David praised her for her wisdom and thanked her for keeping him from shedding innocent blood. David accepted her offering and told her to go home.

When Abigail returned home, she found Nabal celebrating and very drunk. She said nothing until the next morning when Nabal was sober. She told him what happened, and he became like a stone. Ten days later, the Lord struck Nabal dead. David then took Abigail as a wife. David also married Ahinoam, and Saul gave David's wife Michal to another man.

Lectio Divina

Spend 8 to 10 minutes in silent contemplation of the following passage:

David had opportunities to kill Saul, but he had such high regard for the Lord that he would not dare to kill one chosen by God. When people hurt us, we most likely will not be tempted to kill them, but we may try to kill their reputation. Everyone created by the Lord is special to God. When we keep that in mind, we can understand why Jesus keeps telling us to forgive our enemies. The enemy we hate is still deeply loved by God.

✠ *What can I learn from this passage?*

Day 3: Saul's Doom (26—28)

One night, while Saul and Abner slept, David and Abishai came into the camp. Abishai stated that the Lord had delivered Saul to him and told David to simply give the word and he would pin Saul to the ground with one blow. David refused, saying that he cannot hurt the Lord's anointed. Only the Lord can strike him dead. David and Abishai took Saul's spear near his head and the water jug and left.

David went off a distance and called to Abner, who awakened, asking who is calling him. David scoffed at Abner for sleeping when he should have been guarding the king. He declared that the guards deserved death because they have not guarded the anointed of the Lord.

Saul recognized David's voice. David asked why Saul is pursuing him. If the Lord incited Saul against David, then let David make an offering pleasing to the Lord in return. If the people incited Saul against him, may they be cursed before the Lord. David showed the king his spear and invited the king to send an attendant to come and get it. Although the Lord delivered Saul into David's hands, David could not lay a hand on the Lord's anointed. Saul blessed David, saying he will succeed at whatever he does.

David went into hiding in Philistine territory with 600 men and was granted asylum. He lived among the Philistines for a year and four months. When he raided a Philistine town, he would kill every inhabitant and take the livestock with him. During this time, when the king of Achish asked him where he fought, he would name an Israelite territory.

The Philistines mustered a force to fight against the Israelites, and Achish told David that they expected him to fight along with them. David acted as though he was happy with the idea and told Achish that he will now see what David and his men can do. Achish appointed David as his permanent bodyguard.

The author adds that Samuel was dead and that Saul had driven all the mediums and diviners out of the land. When Saul saw the Philistines ready for war, he became afraid and wanted to consult the Lord, but the Lord gave him no answer. Saul told his men to find him a medium, and they spoke of a woman at Endor. He disguised himself, putting on different clothes, and went to the woman at night with two companions. She did not recognize him as the king. When Saul asked her to conjure up a spirit for him, she asked if he wanted to get her killed, since King Saul had expelled all mediums and diviners from the land. Saul promised that she would not be harmed, and he asked her to conjure up Samuel.

When Samuel appeared, the woman shrieked, knowing now that it was Saul who was with her. Saul told her not to be afraid and asked her what she saw. She says that she saw an old man coming up wrapped in a robe. Saul knew that it was Samuel. Samuel then asked Saul why he disturbed him by conjuring him up. Saul told of the war with the Philistines and noted that God no longer answered him through prophets or dreams. Samuel asked why Saul sought help from him if the Lord abandoned Saul. He told him that the Lord had done as Samuel predicted while he lived. He tore the kingdom from Saul and gave it to his neighbor, David. Samuel referred back to Saul's sin of not killing Amalek and keeping the spoils of the battle. Samuel predicted that on the following day, Saul and his son, Jonathan, would be with him and that the army of Israel would be delivered into the hands of the Philistines.

Saul then fell to the ground in fear since he lacked strength from not having eaten all day. The woman reminded Saul that she had obeyed him and carried out his request. She and his two companions convinced Saul to take something to eat.

Lectio Divina

Spend 8 to 10 minutes in silent contemplation of the following passage:

Saul learned that he was to die the next day, and, overcome by fear, he refused to eat. The fear of death was as bad as death itself. Many sinners, knowing that they may be discovered and punished if caught, must often pay the consequences of their sins. Sin may lead the sinner into anxiety, fear, and guilt.

✠ *What can I learn from this passage?*

Day 4: Death of Saul and His Sons (29—31)

As the Philistines were marching toward battle, the commanders of the Philistines asked what the Hebrews were doing as companions of Achish and refused to allow them to fight with them. The commanders feared that the Hebrews, in the middle of the battle, would turn against the Philistines.

While David and his men were away, the Amalekites invaded the land and took captive all in the city, young and old. David and his men found the city burned to the ground, and they pursued the invaders, the Amalekites. Two hundred of his 600 men were too exhausted to continue the journey with him.

David and his army came across an Egyptian who was a slave of the Amalekites and was starving. They gave him food, and he agreed to lead them to the Amalekites, but he wanted assurance that they would not kill him. He led them to the place where the Amalekites were lounging on the ground, eating, drinking, and celebrating their good fortune. David attacked them, and they fought from dawn to Sunday with his 400 men. David's army recovered everything and took the plunder belonging to the Amelekites.

When David and his army returned to the 200 who were too exhausted to continue, some of those who fought refused to share their plunder with them, but David made a law that all share equally.

Saul and his three sons—Jonathan, Abinadab, and Malchishua—suffered a shocking defeat at the hands of the Philistines. In the battle, the Philistines killed Saul's three sons, and an archer severely wounded Saul. Knowing that he would be tortured and humiliated if captured by the Philistines, Saul ordered his armor-bearer to pierce him with the armor-bearer's sword. The terrified armor-bearer refused, so Saul took his own sword and fell upon it. When the armor-bearer saw this, he too took his sword and fell upon it.

Besides the livestock and possessions of the people in cities, the spoils of victory included the weapons and armor of those slain. The day after the battle, when the Philistines came to strip the corpses of the Israelites, they found the bodies of Saul and his three sons. They cut off the head of Saul and stripped him of his armor, sending these throughout the land of the Philistines to bring the good news of Saul's defeat to the people. They placed Saul's armor in the temple of their god and impaled Saul's body on the wall.

Upon hearing that Saul's body was impaled on a wall, some warriors from Jabesh traveled through the night and removed the bodies of Saul and his sons from the wall. Although cremation was not a custom in Israel, the people of Jabesh burned the bodies, most likely due to their wasted condition. They buried the bones and fasted in mourning for seven days. The need to give a respectful burial to Saul and his sons could stem from the city's gratitude to Saul for saving them from the Ammonites in the early days of his reign (see 1 Samuel 11).

Lectio Divina

Spend 8 to 10 minutes in silent contemplation of the following passage:

During his life, Saul sinned against the Lord. On the battlefield, he paid the price for his sins, which led to the deaths of his sons and many in his army. The Lord abandoned Saul in battle. The reality is that sinners do not suffer their fate alone. Many good people, like Jonathan, die with the sinner. Sin not only hurts the one who sins but many others along the way. Jesus came to bring life, but sinners put him to death. Christianity teaches that sin may hurt both the community as well as individuals. We can, however, look forward to an eternal reward if we remain faithful to God.

✠ *What can I learn from this passage?*

Review Questions

1. What was the warning that Jonathan gave to David concerning his father's desire to kill David?
2. Why did Saul slaughter the priests for giving the sacred bread to David and his army?
3. What was David's attitude toward Saul?
4. How would you apply David's law about sharing the plunder with those too weary to fight to areas of our lives today?

The Book of Second Samuel (I)

2 SAMUEL 1—10

And the LORD said to you (David): You shall shepherd my people, Israel; you shall be ruler over Israel (5:2).

Opening Prayer (SEE PAGE 16)

Context

Part 1: 2 Samuel 1—3:1 Saul and Jonathan have been killed in battle, and David grieves for them. David is anointed king of Judah, while Ishbaal is made king of Israel. Abner, a captain from Saul's army, supports Ishbaal. He later kills Asahel, the brother of Joab. Abner and Joab make a truce.

Part 2: 2 Samuel 3:2—10:27 Abner and Ishbaal are killed, and David is made king of Israel. David captures Jerusalem and makes it the religious center of all of Israel by bringing the ark there. Later, Nathan informs David that he will not be allowed to build a house for the Lord, but that the Lord will build him a house, meaning that his family will continue to lead as kings after his death. David takes care of Jonathan's son, Meribbaal, who is disabled.

PART 1: GROUP STUDY (2 SAMUEL 1—3:1)

Read aloud 2 Samuel 1—3:1.

1:1–17 David Learns of the Death of Saul and Jonathan

A man in torn clothing, with dirt on his head, rushed up to David, fell on his face in homage, and announced that Saul and Jonathan were killed. He added that he came upon Saul, wounded and leaning on his spear just as the enemy drew close to him. Since Saul realized that he was near death, he told the man to kill him. The man informed David that he killed Saul as requested. He said that he took the crown on Saul's head and the armlet on his arm and brought them to David.

The story of the man who killed Saul differs from the story found toward the end of 1 Samuel, where Saul kills himself by falling on his own sword. The event is apparently an added source used by the final editor of the Deuteronomistic History, or the man may be lying, hoping to receive a reward from David for saving Saul from a more terrible form of death.

David and his men immediately went into mourning, tearing their clothes, an act that symbolizes mourning in Scripture. Throughout the day, they wept and fasted, mourning for Saul, his son, the army, and the people of Israel. David had the messenger killed, stating that the man had testified against himself in admitting that he was the one who killed the Lord's anointed. David intoned a lamentation over Saul and Jonathan and ordered that all the people of Judah learn the lament. The lament speaks of Saul being slain and orders that the news not reach the Philistines to avoid rejoicing among the Philistine women.

2—3:1 David's Reign in Judah

David asked the Lord if he should go up to the cities of Judah, and the Lord told him to go up to the Hebron, which was a major stronghold in Judah. David, his two wives, and his army with their families traveled to the town of Hebron. The men of Judah anointed David as king, but David still needed to secure support for his kingship. When he heard that the people of Jabesh had buried Saul, he blessed the people and promised that he will show favor to them. He was not only praising them, but he was also using the occasion to solidify his kingship.

At the time Judah anointed David king, the northern and southern tribes of the Israelites were not united. Abner, a captain in Saul's army, refused to accept David as king and installed a forty-year-old son of Saul named Ishbaal as king of the northern kingdom. A confusing episode follows when the armies of Abner and Ishbaal confront the army of Joab, a son of David's sister Zeruiah. The First Book of Chronicles identifies Zeruiah as David's sister (1 Chronicles 2:16). Abner suggests to Joab that their men entertain them by having twelve of them fight each other by grasping each other's head while thrusting their swords into his opponent's side. The fighters all died together, and the place received the name "Field of Sides."

The contest quickly developed into a battle between the two sides. David's warriors defeated Abner and his men, and Abner fled. Three sons of David's sister, Zeruiah, joined in the battle. When Abner fled, one of the sons, Asahel, who was as fast as a gazelle, chased after Abner. Abner begged Asahel to stop, fearing that he would be forced to kill Asahel. He wondered how he could show his face to Joab, Asahel's brother, after killing Asahel, who was not as accomplished in battle as Abner. When Asahel refused to turn away, Abner turned and thrust his spear through him.

Review Questions

1. Why was David first anointed king of Judah and not king of all of Israel?
2. What caused Abner to support Ishbaal, the son of Saul, as king of Israel?
3. Why did Abner wish to avoid killing Asahel, the brother of Joab?

Closing Prayer (SEE PAGE 16)

Pray the closing prayer now or after *lectio divina.*

Lectio Divina (SEE PAGE 9)

Relax your body and maintain a posture of prayer (back straight, eyes shut, feet flat on the floor). This exercise can take as long as you want, but in the context of this Bible study, 10 to 20 minutes should be sufficient.

The meditations that follow are provided only to help group participants use this prayer form, but note that *lectio* is intended to bring one to a place of prayerful contemplation where the Word of God speaks to the hearer from his or her heart. (See page 9 for further instruction.)

David Learns of the Death of Saul and Jonathan (1:1–17)

A woman who gave food to the poor received word from a health official that she could no longer give out food since the date on the food had expired. If she gave it out, she could be arrested and fined. When she explained to an obviously hungry man that she was not allowed to give out any more food, he beat her so badly that she had to be hospitalized. There is an old saying: "Don't kill the messenger." Some people insult ticket collectors who tell them that their flight has been canceled due to inclement weather. The ticket collector and the woman giving out the food are only the messengers. David killed the messenger who told him of Saul's death.

✠ *What can I learn from this passage?*

David's Reign in Judah (2—3:1)

Although the Lord has chosen David to be king, he does not gain control of his kingdom without fighting for it. When God chooses someone for some particular task in creation, God does not necessarily remove all obstacles hindering the fulfillment of God's plan. For example, God inspired Saint Francis of Assisi to serve the poor, but Francis found himself locked away for a period of time and finally disowned by his father. Despite the obstacles he endured in reaching his goals, he was chosen by God to establish a religious order which would eventually have an enormous influence in bringing the message of Christ to continents throughout the world.

✠ *What can I learn from this passage?*

PART 2: INDIVIDUAL STUDY (2 SAMUEL 3:2—10:27)

Day 1: The Fall of Ishbaal (3:2—4:12)

The author lists the six sons of David born to his six wives while he was at Hebron. In David's day, having more than one wife was a custom among rich rulers. Saul had a concubine named Rizpah. Besides their wives, many rulers had concubines who were slaves purchased for sexual relations. Ishbaal accused Abner of sleeping with his father's concubine, which was akin to accusing him of the serious crime of usurping the throne of Saul. Abner asked if Ishbaal considered him to be a dog's head from Judah, a derogatory term used to designate the lowest of the low.

Abner did not deny Ishbaal's accusation, but he angrily reminded Ishbaal that he protected him, his family, and his friends against David. Abner swore before the Lord that he will take away the kingdom of the house of Saul and establish the throne of David over Israel (the northern tribes) as well as Judah. David will reign from Dan to Beer-sheba, which is a reference to the farthest points north and south of the land inhabited by the tribes. Abner has become so powerful that Ishbaal feared him and could no longer speak with authority over him.

Abner sent messengers to David, asking him to enter into a covenant with him. He declared that he would bring all of Israel over to him. David agreed, but a condition of the covenant would be that Michal, Saul's daughter, would be returned to him. It is through Michal that David has become a son-in-law of Saul and through her he receives the right as an heir to Saul's kingdom. Abner took her away from her husband who tracked behind her weeping. Abner ordered him bluntly to go home, which he wisely did.

Abner realized that many of the people wanted David as their king, and the Lord promised that it would be through David that the Philistines would be defeated. Abner had to gain the agreement of the Benjaminites, who would be the most reluctant to accept David, since Saul and Abner both belonged to their tribe. They would not look kindly on someone from another tribe becoming their king. Abner and twenty of his men came to Hebron and dined with David, an act which is a sign of acceptance and friendship.

When Joab learned that David met with Abner and allowed him to leave in peace, Joab angrily confronted David, saying that Abner was using the event as a ruse to learn about David's plans for battle (referred to as his "comings and goings" in the Bible). Joab hated Abner since Abner killed his brother, Asahel.

Unknown to David, Joab sent messengers to Abner to meet with him at Hebron. When Abner returned to Hebron, Joab stabbed him in the abdomen. When David heard about Abner's death, he had to assure those who heard about it that he and his kingdom are innocent of Abner's blood. He cursed Joab and his family, placing them under a shadow of continual suffering that involved a number of ailments or tragedies.

David visibly mourned Abner, tearing his garments and putting on sackcloth, a symbol of mourning. He followed the bier and wept aloud with all the people at the grave of Abner. The people wanted to console David with food, but David swore that he would not eat anything before sunset. All that David did met the approval of the people, and they were convinced that the king had nothing to do with Abner's death.

Ishbaal lost courage when he heard that Abner was dead at Hebron and that the people of Israel were distressed. Two of Ishbaal's company leaders snuck past Ishbaal's gatekeeper while she was asleep, entered Ishbaal's bedroom, and while he slept, cut off his head. The author mentions that Jonathan had a son named Meribbaal, whose nurse dropped him when he was five years old and injured him.

The company leaders took Ishbaal's head and traveled all night to bring it to David, expecting David to give them a reward for killing Ishbaal. Instead, David treated them as he treated the man who brought him news of Saul's death. He referred to them as wicked men who killed an innocent man in his bed. David followed a ritual used for traitors, having them killed, cutting off their hands and feet, and hanging them. David buried the head of Ishbaal.

Lectio Divina

Spend 8 to 10 minutes in silent contemplation of the following passage:

The Scriptures refer to David as a man after the Lord's own heart, which meant that the Lord loved David very much. The Lord's love for David offers a source of hope to all people. David was very human, a sinner, and a lover. Many lovers of God are also men and women who have failed to live up to all that God asks of them. David's human strengths and weaknesses encourage us to live close to God, despite our weaknesses and failures.

✠ *What can I learn from this passage?*

Day 2: David in Jerusalem (5—6)

Since David was already anointed king of Judah in an earlier episode, the northern tribes (Israel) announced that they accept him as king because they are related to David. All the tribes share a common ancestry, going back to Jacob, the father of the twelve sons of Israel. At Hebron, David made a covenant with Israel, and they anointed him king of Israel. David was now king of all of the Israelites.

The Jebusites lived in Jerusalem before the Israelites entered the Promised Land. Jerusalem provided the most strategic area for the capital of the Israelite nation. It was on the border between the northern and southern tribes yet belonged to neither side. In choosing to capture Jerusalem, a neutral city, David shrewdly avoided any show of favoritism. David and his army attacked the Jebusites and captured the city.

David moved his kingdom from Hebron to Jerusalem. The king of Tyre sent cedar wood, carpenters, and masons to build David's house. David's kingdom became a glorious kingdom, not only for the sake of David himself but for all of Israel. He took many concubines and wives in Jerusalem and became the father of many more sons and daughters. The number of concubines and wives often stressed the exalted position of the king.

When the Philistines heard that David was anointed king over all of Israel, they confronted him in battle. David sought counsel from the Lord, and the Lord directed him to battle the Philistines, promising to deliver them into the hands of the Israelites. David and his men carried off the images of the gods abandoned by the retreating Philistines. In war, the victorious army would confiscate the images of the gods of the defeated army to show that their own god was more powerful. Taking the images of the Philistine gods is in contrast to the earlier episode where the Philistines captured the ark.

The Philistines confronted the Israelites at Rephaim, and the Lord directed David not to attack them from the front but to circle around behind them. When the wind blew through the trees, it would sound like a marching army. Then the Israelites did as directed and routed the Philistines.

David chose 30,000 men to accompany him in transporting the Ark of the Covenant from Judah to Jerusalem. Two sons of Abinadab named Uzzah and Ahio guided the ark on a new cart from the house of Abinadab, while David and all of Israel danced before the ark, singing and playing instruments. At one point, the oxen were tipping the ark and Uzzah reached out to steady it. The ark was so sacred that the Lord struck Uzzah dead for attempting to touch it. When David saw this, he became so frightened that he left the ark at the house of a man named Obed-edom instead of bringing it into Jerusalem.

For three months, the ark remained in the house of Obed-edom and the Lord blessed him and his household. When David heard of the blessings bestowed on Obed-edom, he went to bring the ark to the city of David. His bearers took the ark, and after they had walked six steps, they stopped and David sacrificed an ox and a fatling. After the sacrifice, they proceeded to Jerusalem.

David led the procession, dancing feverishly before the ark, wearing only an ephod, which, in this case, resembled a nightshirt. When they entered Jerusalem, Michal, David's wife and the daughter of Saul, looked out the window and saw David dancing nearly naked before the ark. She felt loathing for him. The procession ended in Jerusalem with David offering sacrifices to the Lord. When David returned home, Michal mocked him, berating him for being a king who exposed himself in view of the slave girls of his followers, as a commoner would do. David replied that he was dancing before the Lord and that he would dance before the Lord again, even if it meant demeaning himself in the eyes of Michal.

By uniting the tribes and choosing Jerusalem for his throne, David made Jerusalem the political capital of Israel. By bringing the ark to Jerusalem, David made Jerusalem the religious capital of Israel. When the passage ends, the author tells us that Michal was childless until the day she died.

Lectio Divina

Spend 8 to 10 minutes in silent contemplation of the following passage:

> David's love for God showed itself as he was willing to make himself a fool for the Lord by dancing before the Ark of the Covenant as it came into Jerusalem. In David's thinking, he may be king, but the real king is the Lord, so he dances before the ark, which symbolizes the presence of God. When a person loves God, that person can appear to be a real fool in the eyes of worldly people, especially when they are willing to make sacrifices or die for Christ.

✠ *What can I learn from this passage?*

Day 3: The House of David (7—8)

The passage begins with the message that the Lord has given David rest from all his enemies. In reality, as we learn in future chapters, David will continue to battle against various enemies. Nathan, a prophet during David's time as a king, learned that David wished to build a house for the ark. David looked around at his house of cedar and reflected that the dwelling place of the Lord is a tent. At first, Nathan tells David to do what he wishes, for the Lord is with him.

Later that night, the word of the Lord came to Nathan, directing him to inform David that the Lord has never dwelt in a house from the day the Lord led the Israelites out of Egypt. This is not entirely true. In 1 Samuel, the author told us about a house of the Lord in Shiloh that was used for worship in the time of Eli (1 Samuel 1–3). These two contradictory stories could come from two separate traditions gathered by the editor of 2 Samuel.

The Lord promised that David's name will be among the greatest on earth. Nathan recalled for David that the Lord settled the people of Israel on a land chosen by the Lord. The Lord promised that they will never be troubled again, and the wicked shall never oppress them, as they did at the beginning and during the time of the judges. The Lord promised to make a house for David, a promise which is a play on the word "house." The house the Lord will build for David will come through his offspring and become the house of David.

The Lord made a reference to a future king who will build a house for the Lord. This is Solomon, who will have the Temple constructed in Jerusalem. The Lord will be a father to him, and he shall be a son to the Lord. If he does wrong, the Lord will punish him with human punishments, that is, allow human beings to punish him, but the Lord will not take the kingship away from him and his offspring as the Lord did to Saul. The house of David and his kingdom is firmly established forever.

The editor strings together a series of David's victories to show that David conquered most of the land promised to the Israelites by the Lord. After the summary of the conquests, the author provides a list of names which includes Joab as the commander of the army, a chancellor, priests, a scribe, and David's sons as priests. The list illustrates that David not only united the Israelites, but he also established an organized administration to govern Israel. The list most likely does not include all administrative offices in Israel.

Lectio Divina

Spend 8 to 10 minutes in silent contemplation of the following passage:

> Among David's offspring is Jesus, the Son of God become human. God's blessing to David is God's blessing to us. Jesus, the Christ, brought salvation to the world and made us heirs of the kingdom of God. We share spiritually in the line of David through Jesus Christ. David's privilege becomes our privilege.

✠ *What can I learn from this passage?*

Day 4: David's Campaign Against Ammon (9—10:27)

Before the death of Jonathan, Saul's son, David made a covenant with him, promising that he (David) would never cut off Jonathan's name from the face of the earth. This meant that David would not kill any male offspring of Jonathan (see 1 Samuel 20:14–17). David asked an official of the house of Saul if there were any survivors in the family of Saul. The official told David that a son of Jonathan, whose feet are disabled, survives (see 2 Samuel 4:4).

David sent for Jonathan's son, Meribbaal, who falls face down in homage before David. Meribbaal may have thought that David was going to kill him. David promised that he would be kind to him for the sake of his father, Jonathan. The term "kind" connotes a fulfillment of a covenant.

David informed Meribbaal that he will restore to him all the lands of Saul, his grandfather, and that he, Meribbaal, will always eat at the table of David. Eating at David's table showed that David favored him. Since Meribbaal legs were injured, he was unable to serve in battle, and as such, was not a likely candidate to serve as a king. David, however, could not trust himself to any unknown rivals, so dining at David's table allowed David to watch Meribbaal, a possible heir to Saul's kingdom. David chose Ziba to care for the land he is giving to Meribbaal. Ziba, who had fifteen sons and twenty servants, was to bring in the produce of the land for Meribbaal's household. He tells Ziba that Meribbaal himself shall eat at the king's table, so Ziba willingly accepts the king's command.

When the king of the Ammonites died, David sent an envoy to the king's son, Hanun, to return a kindness the king had shown him. The princes of the Ammonites warned the new king that David was sending spies, not an envoy in peace. When the envoy arrived, the king had their beards shaved and their tunics cut off halfway to the hips. He then sent them away. Upon receiving news of this disgrace to his men, David sent messengers to intercept them, telling them to remain at Jericho until their beards grew back.

When the Ammonites realized that they had offended David and would surely have to fight the Israelites, they called upon the Arameans to support them in battle against them. The Israelites came out to battle and found that the Ammonites set up their army at the city gate, and those supporting them set up their armies in the field. This meant that Joab, David's commander, faced an army in front of him and another in back of him. Joab split his men into two fighting groups and placed Abishai, another leader, in charge of one group while he led the other. Each one faced the enemy and eventually defeated them.

The kings of the Arameans were forced to make peace with the Israelites by becoming their subjects, as they were too terrified to give further support to the Ammonites.

Lectio Divina

Spend 8 to 10 minutes in silent contemplation of the following passage:

When David treats Jonathan's injured son with respect, he is fulfilling a promise that he would not harm Jonathan's offspring. Despite all his weaknesses, David was a man of honor when it came to loving the Lord and keeping the commitments he made in life. Jesus himself viewed faithfulness to a promise to be so important that he said, "Let your 'Yes' mean 'Yes,' and your 'No' mean 'No.' Anything more is from the evil one" (Matthew 5:37).

✠ *What can I learn from this passage?*

Review Questions

1. Why did David mourn the death of Abner?
2. What caused David to pass a sentence of death on the men who killed Ishbaal?
3. How is the Lord planning to build a house for David?
4. Why did David fear leaving Meribbaal out of his sight?

The Book of Second Samuel (II)

2 SAMUEL 11–24

The LORD lives! Blessed be my rock! Exalted be God, the rock of my salvation (22:47).

Opening Prayer (SEE PAGE 16)

Context

Part 1: 2 Samuel 11—12 David impregnates Bathsheba and David has her husband, Uriah, killed. Using a parable, Nathan makes David admit guilt in the death of Uriah, and Nathan informs him that the Lord forgives him, but the child of Bathsheba will die.

Part 2: 2 Samuel 13—24 Amnon rapes his half-sister Tamar and is killed by Absalom, who flees from David. Using a parable, a woman makes David face his guilt and welcome Absalom back. Absalom has himself crowned king and forces David to flee from Jerusalem. Judah again accepts David as king when Absalom is killed. David sins by calling for a census, and the Lord sends a plague to all of Israel.

PART 1: GROUP STUDY (2 SAMUEL 11—12)

Read aloud 2 Samuel 11—12.

11:1–27 The Result of David's Sins

One evening, David was strolling on the roof of his house, which was built higher than other houses, affording David a view of the rooftops of the houses below. From this vantage point, David saw a beautiful woman bathing. David sent people to learn who the woman was, and they returned with the news that she was Bathsheba, wife of Uriah the Hittite, who was Joab's armor-bearer. David took her to his bed at a time when she had just purified after her period. Bathsheba became pregnant and sent a messenger to inform David.

David immediately set about covering up his sin. He sent a message to Joab, telling him to send Uriah to him. When Uriah arrived, David plied him with questions about the battles as though this was the reason for having him come. Uriah answered that all was going well. David then told Uriah to go to his house and bathe his feet, which is a euphemism for sexual relations. When Uriah left David, a portion was sent to him from the king's table. Uriah, however, slept at the entrance to the king's house with David's other officers. The officers told David that Uriah had not gone to his house.

When David asked Uriah why he did not go to his house, Uriah answered that he cannot go home and eat, drink, and sleep with his wife while the ark, Joab, and the army were dwelling in tents in the open field. On the following day, he invited Uriah to eat and drink with him, and Uriah became drunk. When he left David, he went to sleep on his bed among David's servants and did not go to his house. The next morning, David wrote a letter to Joab telling him to place Uriah in a position where the fighting was most intense, and then to pull back and leave Uriah where he will be killed. He sent Uriah to Joab with the letter, knowing that Uriah would not dare read his message. Joab placed Uriah at a point where he knew he would be killed. Uriah and some officers of David's army were killed.

Joab apparently blundered in the attack by allowing his men to get too close to the city wall. David wanted Uriah killed, but not the other men. Joab sent a report of the battle to David, telling his messengers that David will become angry because they were too close to the wall. He said that David will recall Abimelech, who was killed near a wall by a woman who threw a millstone on his head (see Judges 9:50–55). Joab wisely told his men that as David is ranting in anger, they are to add that Uriah, the Hittite, was also dead.

The messengers reported to David as Joab directed. Instead of becoming angry, David encouraged Joab, telling him not to be discouraged by this evil, since the deaths coming from battle are never predictable. He sent word to Joab to reinforce his attack on the city and destroy it.

12:1–31 Nathan's Parable

The Lord sent Nathan to David with a parable about a rich man with a large number of flocks and herds who took the ewe lamb from a poor man to feed a visitor. The poor man nourished the ewe, which grew up with him and his children. He shared the little he had with the ewe, who drank from his cup. The ewe slept against him and was like a daughter to him. The rich man did not take from his own flock but took the poor man's ewe.

David became angry and said to Nathan that the man deserves death. He must make restitution fourfold for the lamb because of his insensitivity. Nathan stunned David when he said, "You are the man!"

Nathan said that because of David's sin, the Lord will not bring peace to David's household. The Lord informed David that he will see his neighbors take his wives and lie with them in broad daylight. David's action was done secretly, but the Lord will punish David in the sight of all Israel.

David accepted that he had indeed sinned, and Nathan told him that the Lord had removed his sin. He will not die, but the child who will be born will die. When the child was born, the child became dreadfully sick, and David begged God for the child, fasting and spending the night in sackcloth as a sign of repentance. No one could appease David. When the child died on the seventh day, David's servants were afraid to tell him, knowing his agony while the child was alive.

When David received the news of the child's death, he rose from the ground, washed and anointed himself, changed his clothes, went to the house of Lord, worshiped, and later ate some food. His surprised servants asked why he went through so much agony when the child was alive, and now that the child has died, he rises and takes food. David said that while the child was alive, there was a possibility that the Lord would listen to him. He cannot bring the child back again. David consoled his wife, Bathsheba, and she conceived and bore a son who received the name Solomon. The Lord loved him and sent the prophet Nathan to name him Jedidiah on behalf of the Lord. The name means "beloved of Yahweh."

In the meanwhile, Joab fought against the Ammonites and captured the royal city. He asked David to assemble the rest of the soldiers and join in the siege of the city and capture it so that people will praise David and not Joab. David joined in the siege and captured the city, taking a crown from an idol and placing it on his own head, showing his power over the idol. He plundered the city and deported the people to work as slaves for his projects.

Review Questions

1. What sins did David commit as a result of Bathsheba's pregnancy? Why?

2. How did Joab displease David when he had Uriah killed?

3. Why did God send Nathan to David with a parable instead of simply telling David that he sinned gravely? How can you apply this parable to your own life today?

Closing Prayer (SEE PAGE 16)

Pray the closing prayer now or after *lectio divina*.

Lectio Divina (SEE PAGE 9)

Relax your body and maintain a posture of prayer (back straight, eyes shut, feet flat on the floor). This exercise can take as long as you want, but in the context of this Bible study, 10 to 20 minutes should be sufficient.

The meditations that follow are provided only to help group participants use this prayer form, but note that *lectio* is intended to bring one to a place of prayerful contemplation where the Word of God speaks to the hearer from his or her heart. (See page 9 for further instruction.)

The Result of David's Sins (11:1–27)

The story of David and Bathsheba and the murder of Uriah offer an insight into the power of sin. Not only does one sin lead to another, but the sin that follows may be far worse than the first sin. Sinners must admit the sin and seek forgiveness, or sinners may easily begin to excuse themselves for any sins that follow. They reason that God does not care if they sin, or that their sin is not enough to condemn them, but this thinking is false and could easily cause them to lose their sense of sin.

✠ *What can I learn from this passage?*

Nathan's Parable (12:1–31)

An eighty-year-old man who repented of his sinful younger life told his pastor that he stepped outside himself and looked on himself as someone else would. He did not like what he saw so, with the grace of God, he confessed his sins and changed his way of life. Nathan's parable to David led David to view himself through the eyes of another. He did not like what he saw and he repented. God forgave David just as God forgives all sinners who truly repent.

✠ *What can I learn from this passage?*

PART 2: INDIVIDUAL STUDY (2 SAMUEL 13—24)

Day 1: Amnon's Rape of Tamar (13—14)

Absalom, one of David's sons, had a sister named Tamar who was very beautiful. Amnon, a half-brother of Absalom, had a friend named Jonadab, a clever nephew of David. Amnon feigned sickness, and David was told that Amnon could eat if Tamar prepared something in Amnon's presence. David sent Tamar to Amnon. When Tamar prepared the meal, Amnon led her into the bedroom and raped her and in the end, he hated her, casting her out of his presence. She begged Amnon not to send her away, since that would be worse than the offense Amnon already committed. Once the rape took place, Tamar could find some dignity if Amnon had kept her as a wife or concubine.

Tamar left, putting ashes on her head and tearing the long tunic she wore as a virgin, both signs of mourning. When Absalom found her weeping, he asked if Amnon had been intimate with her. Learning what had happened, Absalom seemed not to care. Tamar remained in Absalom's house.

When David heard about the situation, he became angry but did nothing, since he loved Amnon, who was his firstborn with the right of succession to the throne. Absalom said nothing to Amnon, but he hated him for having humiliated his sister.

Two years later, when it was sheep-shearing time, Absalom invited all the king's sons to a festival. At the time of sheep-shearing, it was customary to celebrate with much eating and drinking. Absalom also invited his father, David, and his servants, but David declined, saying that his coming would put a burden on Absalom. Absalom's purpose in having the brothers come was to gain the confidence of Amnon so he could kill him. It is not clear why he invited David, although he may already be planning to kill David, since he (Absalom) would be next in line after Amnon as an heir to the throne. Absalom prepared a huge feast and told his attendants to watch for the time when Amnon was merry with wine. Absalom will give the order to kill him, which they are to do. Absalom told them not to fear since he was the one who ordered them to do this deed.

When the attendants killed Amnon, the other brothers mounted their mules and fled. While they were still on the road, word came to David that Absalom has killed all his sons. The king, in mourning, tore his clothes and fell to the ground, and all his servants did the same. Jonadab informed David that only Amnon was killed and that his other sons were safe. In the meanwhile, Absalom fled.

The king's sons returned to David and all wept loudly over the death of Amnon. Absalom remained away for three years. Joab brought a wise woman to David from a town south of Bethlehem. She was to act as though she were in mourning. Wise in the biblical sense could mean skillful, which implies that the woman would be skillful enough to convince David that she was truly in mourning.

When the woman came to David, she paid the usual homage by falling on the ground before him and asked his help in judging her case. She posed as a widow who had two sons, but one of the sons killed the other in an argument. Just as Nathan came before David with a parable about a rich man with many sheep taking the ewe lamb of a poor man to feed a guest in order to have David pass judgment on himself, so the woman's aim is to have David condemn himself. The woman claims that the clan seeks the death of her other son, which would mean that all the heirs of her deceased husband would be eliminated and her husband would have no name or posterity, a horrible penalty for an Israelite. Since David had other sons, the story did not apply to him fully, but the author seems to ignore this fact.

When someone kills another, an avenger, who is often a member of the clan, seeks his death. David promised that not a hair of her son's head will fall to the ground, a command from David that no one shall hurt or kill her son. The woman then turned the story on David, saying that he is guilty of not bringing back his own banished son, who is Absalom, and the woman insisted that God has devised ways to avoid banishing anyone. The woman compared life to water poured on the ground which cannot be gathered up again. This was a reference to Amnon who was dead and cannot come back to life.

David, recognizing the ruse as coming from someone favorable to Absalom, makes the woman admit that Joab instructed her to come to him and speak in this manner. David told Joab that he had accepted his request to allow Absalom to return. When Joab brought Absalom to Jerusalem, the king still refused to see him.

Two years after Absalom arrived in Jerusalem, he twice sent word to Joab to bring him to the king, but Joab did not answer him. Absalom sent his servants to burn Joab's fields. When Joab learned that Absalom had burned his field because he (Joab) would not bring him to the king, Joab reported all that happened to David. David invited Absalom to come to him. When Absalom arrived, he fell before David in homage, and David kissed him, a sign of forgiveness. Although all seemed well between David and Absalom, it would soon be clear that Absalom had other ambitions.

Lectio Divina

Spend 8 to 10 minutes in silent contemplation of the following passage:

David continues to show himself to be a man of many contradictions, weeping over the death of his enemies, repenting over his order to have Uriah killed, refusing to see his son, Absalom, for two years, and finally forgiving Absalom when he meets him. He is a lover of the Lord, seeking to live faithfully, but he has an abundance of weaknesses. Through all his sinful deeds, however, he never loses faith in the Lord, trusting that the Lord will forgive him when he seeks forgiveness. And the Lord always forgives him.

✠ *What can I learn from this passage?*

Day 2: Absalom's Plans for Kingship (15—17)

Absalom began to act like a king, taking chariots, horses, and fifty men. He shrewdly placed himself in a position on the road where he would meet people bringing a case before the king and hint that he should be appointed judge, which is the duty of a king. He would embrace and kiss those who gave him homage, gradually ingratiating himself with the people.

Absalom asked David to allow him to go to Hebron to fulfill a vow he made while in exile from David. Unknown to David, Absalom sent word throughout the tribes of Israel that when they hear the sound of the horn, they were to declare that Absalom was king in Hebron, the original capital of Judah, where David was anointed king.

Absalom became powerful and was about to attack Jerusalem, making David and his army flee with his entire household. He left only ten of his concubines behind to care for the palace. David left the Ark of the Covenant in the city, saying that if he returned, it would be a sign that the Lord was with him, and if he does not, he is willing to accept whatever the Lord had in store for him. David was especially saddened to learn that Ahithophel, a beloved advisor, had joined Absalom.

When David and his army reached the top of the Mount of Olives, he met a man named Hushai, who was in mourning. David sent him back to Jerusalem to act as a spy, feigning allegiance to Absalom. He was to pass on what he learns from Absalom to the priests who would contact David. So David's friend Hushai went to Jerusalem to join Absalom.

Ziba met David on the Mount of Olives with saddled donkeys, 200 loaves of bread, cakes of pressed raisins, summer fruits, and a skin of wine. He told David that the gifts are for David and his men to sustain them on their journey. Ziba also informed David that Jonathan's son, Meribbaal, remained in Jerusalem, hoping that the Israelites would anoint him as the rightful king. David gave Meribbaal's possessions and land to Ziba.

Shimei, a man from the same clan as Saul, began cursing the king and his officers, throwing stones and dirt at them. He accused David of being a man of blood and shouted that he was being paid back for all the blood he spilled from the family of Saul and for taking the kingdom. Abishai, one of the brothers of Joab and a son of David's sister, Zeruiah, called Shimei a dead dog and asked David to allow him to lop off Shimei's head. David refused to kill the man, saying that the Lord sent him and perhaps the Lord will bless David for accepting these curses without performing an evil act.

In the meanwhile, Absalom, with all his Israelite followers, and Ahithophel, who once counseled David, entered Jerusalem. When Absalom met Hushai, he questioned Hushai about his allegiance to David. Hushai stated that he belonged to the one the Lord had chosen and that he will remain with Absalom. In reality, he believed that the Lord has chosen David and, unknown to Absalom, he was remaining faithful to the one the Lord had chosen, namely David.

Absalom asked Ahithophel for counsel about asserting his kingship, and Ahithophel directed him to take David's concubines for himself. Absalom set up a tent on his roof and took David's concubines in view of all the people. Sharing sexually with the king's concubines symbolized a claim to the throne. When the people see that Absalom has treated David with such contempt, his followers will become courageous, since they will recognize it as Absalom's claim to kingship. Recall how Nathan came to David in an earlier passage and declared that the Lord will repay David for his sin with Bathsheba and Uriah, predicting that David's secret sin will be repaid in a manner for all the people to see (2 Samuel 12:12).

Ahithophel gave a second counsel to Absalom, asking to choose 12,000 men to pursue David, who would be weary and disheartened. Ahithophel believed that his attack would cause David's followers to panic, and he promised to kill only the king. He will bring back the followers of David as a bride returns to her husband. And he counseled Absalom that through the death of one person peace might come to all the people. Absalom and the elders approved of the idea.

Absalom and the elders sent for Hushai to hear what he had to say. Hushai disagreed with Ahithophel's counsel, saying that David is leading a fierce force of fighting men and that David himself will not sleep with the army but will be hidden in one of the caves in the area or some other place. If some of the fighters with Ahithophel were killed, the people will say that Absalom's followers have been slaughtered. Hushai said that Absalom should gather an immense force from one end of Israel to the other and lead them himself. With this large force, Absalom will be able to slaughter them all.

Absalom and all the Israelites agreed that Hushai's plan sounded better. In reality, Hushai's plan was to warn David and give him time to escape a trap. The author states that the Lord ordained that the better counsel of Ahithophel should be rejected so that the Lord may bring Absalom to destruction.

Hushai, as planned, reported the situation to the priests, Zadok and Abiathar, who brought the news to a maidservant to bring it to the sons of Zadok and Abiathar, who were to finally bring it to David. The sons of the priests reached David and urged him to quickly cross the Jordan with his people, which they did.

Ahithophel, seeing that his counsel was not accepted, saddled his donkey and went to his home. At home, he left orders concerning his family and hanged himself. The author gives no reason for Ahithophel's decision to hang himself. It could be that he realized that the end of Absalom was near or that he felt rebuked by Absalom and would no longer be trusted, since the Lord was obviously not with him.

Absalom crossed the Jordan with all of Israel. In the meanwhile, a man named Barzillai brought some men who provided beds, covers, food, and drink for David's army.

Lectio Divina

Spend 8 to 10 minutes in silent contemplation of the following passage:

> When Absalom challenged David, many of David's followers who previously supported him suddenly abandoned him. The lesson of the passage touches on a reality of life, namely that we can expect many good moments in our life, but they can also be followed by difficult ones. On Palm Sunday, crowds cheered as Jesus entered Jerusalem. On Good Friday, many of the same people called for his crucifixion. David and Jesus teach us a lesson about remaining faithful to our mission, both in good and difficult times.

> ✠ *What can I learn from this passage?*

Day 3: The Death of Absalom (18—19)

As the armies prepared to fight Absalom, the leaders persuaded David not to go into battle with them, since he is the one the enemy wanted to kill. David agreed and asked them in the hearing of the soldiers to be gentle with his young son, Absalom, thus showing that David had nothing to do with the death of his son.

David chose a thick forest for the battle to counter any form of united attack from the troops of Absalom. In the battle, Absalom, whose long hair was his pride, was caught by his hair as he passed under a tree. His mule kept moving, leaving Absalom swinging by his hair. The Israelites considered a mule to be a mount for a king. Absalom's humiliating loss of his mount could symbolize Absalom's loss of the kingship.

One of Joab's men saw Absalom hanging by his hair and reported it to Joab, who asked why the man did not kill Absalom. Joab told him that he would have rewarded him with fifty pieces of silver if he had killed Absalom. The man said that even if he were offered a thousand pieces of silver, he would not lay a hand on Absalom since he heard the order given by David that they protect him. If it became known to David, the man said that Joab would stand by doing and saying nothing in his defense when David killed him.

Joab dislodged Absalom from the tree, and ten warriors joined in killing Absalom. Since ten were involved, no one person could be accused of killing

Absalom. Joab sounded the horn, ending the battle. They buried Absalom in a deep pit and covered it with a large mound of stones, a symbol used in the case of a person who has been cursed.

Ahimaaz, son of Zadok, wanted to run to David with word that he believed would be good news for the king. Joab refused to send him. He knew that news of the death of Absalom would not be received well by David. Instead, he sent a Cushite, but Ahimaaz kept pestering Joab, who finally relented and told him to go. Ahimaaz ran and reached the king first. He paid homage to David and praised the Lord for wiping out those who rebelled against David. When the Cushite arrived right after Ahimaaz with news of the victory, he told David that Absalom was killed. Upon realizing that Absalom was dead, David retreated to a room over the city and wept over his son's death, wishing that he had died instead.

When Joab and others heard that the king was weeping for Absalom, the whole army joined in mourning, turning the victory celebration into grieving. The soldiers slink into the city, as ashamed as if they lost the battle. Joab berated David, telling him that he shamed his army by showing more love for those who hated him. Joab accused David of hating those who love him. He sarcastically adds that David would not be disturbed if Absalom were alive and all of David's soldiers were killed. He strongly urged David to go out and speak kindly to his army, lest no one will remain faithful to him overnight, which would be a greater disaster for David and those connected to him. David went out and sat at the gate, a symbol that he had taken his place as king. When the people heard this, they trusted that they could come into his presence.

After strengthening his hold on Judah, David made Amasa, Absalom's general, the commander of David's troops to win even favorable support from Absalom's troops. At the Jordan, many people of Judah came to meet David. Shimei, who cursed David and threw rocks and dirt at him, rushed to greet him along with a thousand men from the tribe of Benjamin, which was the tribe to which Saul belonged. Abishai, the son of David's sister, Zeruiah, wanted to kill Shimei, but David rebuked him and questioned why anyone should die on the day when he is recognized as king of Israel.

Ziba, with his fifteen sons and twenty servants, also rushed to the Jordan. Meribbaal also came to David, saying that he had not cared for his feet, trimmed his mustache, or washed his clothes, a sign that he was in mourning over David's need to leave Jerusalem. He reported that he wished to join David earlier, but Ziba, his servant, slandered the king and left him. David, not knowing whether Ziba or Meribbaal were lying, decided to split the land between the two of them.

Barzillai—who provided beds, covers, food, and drink to David and his men while they were fleeing from Absalom (see 2 Samuel 17:27–29)— came to David at the Jordan. The king asked him to travel with him as his guest in Jerusalem, but Barzillai said that he was now an old man who cannot taste what he eats and drinks or hear the voices of the men and women singers. His only wish was to go back and die in his own city by the tomb of his parents, so he requested that David allow his son Chimham to cross with him. After the others had crossed the Jordan, David crossed, accompanied by Chimham.

An argument ensued between Judah (the southern tribe) and the Israelites (the ten northern tribes) over escorting the king across the waters. Both wanted to be first in leading him, with the people of Judah saying that David belonged to their tribe and the people of Israel arguing that their tribes came from sons who were older than Judah. Their argument was fierce, showing that the link between the northern tribes and Judah was unstable. This would have dire consequences for the later history of the Israelite nation.

Lectio Divina

Spend 8 to 10 minutes in silent contemplation of the following passage:

David showed his worthiness to lead when he kept his soldiers from killing Shimei, who came cursing and throwing dirt at him. David saw the Lord's hand in this and all that happened to him. His faith becomes an example for all of us to trust the Lord and to recognize that the Lord is with us in good times and bad.

✠ *What can I learn from this passage?*

Day 4: David's Song of Gratitude (20—21)

Sheba, a Benjaminite, called the people to leave David's leadership and follow him. The author says that all the Israelites left David to follow Sheba, but the rest of the story does not support this. The people of Judah remained loyal to David. David placed the ten concubines whom Absalom raped in plain sight of the people under guard. David provided for their needs, but he never saw them again, making them live the rest of their lives as though they were widows.

Joab, now one of the leaders pursuing Sheba, met Amasa, David's new commander, on the road. He leaned toward Amasa as though to kiss him, and, holding Amasa by the beard, he plunged his sword into the abdomen of the unsuspecting Amasa. Joab may not have trusted Amasa, or he may have become jealous of him, since Joab himself wanted to be the commander of David's armies.

Sheba led his troops to a city in the northern part of Israel. When Joab's troops threatened the city with destruction and were battering its thick walls, a woman, who apparently held some official position within the city, called out for Joab to speak with her. Joab explained that he does not wish to swallow up the city or batter down its walls, but he was seeking Sheba, who has rebelled against King David. Joab told her to surrender Sheba and they will leave. The woman promised to send Sheba's head over the wall of the city, which she did. Joab led his troops home. Now that Amasa was dead, Joab was the commander of the whole army of Israel.

A three-year famine plagued the city. The Lord informed David that there was a blood-guilt on Saul and his family because Saul put the Gibeonites to death. The Gibeonites were not Israelites but survivors of the Amorites and, despite an oath made with the Israelites, Saul tried to slaughter all the Gibeonites. David asked the Gibeonites what he must do to appease them, and they requested seven men from among the descendants of Saul so that they may be executed in the land of the Gibeonites. The king surrendered the seven, sparing only Meribbaal, the son of Jonathan. Two of Saul's sons and five grandsons were turned over to these Gibeonites, who executed them on a mountain before the Lord.

The story of the killing of the seven members of Saul seems to belong at the beginning of chapter nine, which began with David asking if there were any survivors of Saul's family. In this current passage, Saul spared Meribbaal. In chapter nine, David learned that Meribbaal was the only survivor of the family of David.

A woman named Rizpah of the tribe of Saul spread out sackcloth for herself on a rock from the beginning of the harvest until it rained, protecting the dead bodies of her sons, fending off birds during the day, and protecting them from wild animals at night. When King David heard about the plight of Rizpah, he took the bones of Saul and Jonathan from the citizens of Jabesh and buried them with those who were executed in the territory of Benjamin. After this, the famine ended.

Lectio Divina

Spend 8 to 10 minutes in silent contemplation of the following passage:

Although David turned over the relatives of Saul to the Gibeonites, he follows one of the strictest practices of the Israelites, namely care for the dead. His action is more than his concern for the woman who protected the corpses of her sons; it is an important sign of respect for the bodies of Saul and his relatives. Respect for the dead is one of the strongest practices in Christianity, since Christians view the body as a temple of the Holy Spirit, worthy of a dignified burial.

✠ *What can I learn from this passage?*

Day 5: David's Song of Thanksgiving (22—24)

David prays words from Psalm 18, which was written long after David's reign. The author attributes the psalm to David since it fits the occasion. The psalm pictures the Lord as a rock for David, a place where David could find shelter, protection (shield), and liberation. In the psalm, David declared that the Lord saved him because the Lord loved him. The Lord recognized the righteousness of David, who was faithful and loyal to God.

For David, the God of the Israelites was indeed the one true Lord, who gave David the skill and ability to fight with dexterity.

The psalm is followed by an oracle that is presented as David's last words. The oracle follows a biblical tradition of ascribing a poem as the last words of great leaders in the Bible, such as Jacob, whose poem spoke about the future of the tribes (Genesis 49), and Moses, whose poem spoke of past and future blessings, warnings, and the power of the Lord (Exodus 32—33:44). The author introduced the oracle by presenting an image of David as a prophet who was exalted, anointed, and favored by God.

David ordered Joab to take a census of Israel and Judah, but Joab attempted to dissuade David from such foolish action. David insisted, and Joab and his men spent nine months and twenty days taking the census. Kings of ancient times would take a census to know the number of men able to fight and the number of people to tax.

David later realized that he had sinned against the Lord by taking the census. The real king of Israel is the Lord, and the Lord alone should be the one to know the number of Israelites. The Lord sent Gad, the prophet, with three options for David to consider as punishment for his sin. Gad told David that he may choose three years of famine, three months of fleeing from his enemy, or three days of a plague in the land. David chose three days of plague, trusting that the plague was in the Lord's hands, and the Lord is a Lord of mercy.

The plague killed 70,000 people. When the angel of the Lord was about to destroy Jerusalem with the plague, the Lord stopped the angel from any more destruction. During the plague, David told the Lord that he, the shepherd of the people, was the one who had sinned, so the Lord should punish him and his household. Gad told David to set up an altar to the Lord on a threshing floor owned by a man named Araunah.

When Araunah saw David and his servants coming, he ran out to meet them and paid homage to the king. Araunah offered to give David the threshing floor and animals for sacrifice, charging him nothing. David insisted on paying, saying that he cannot offer sacrifices to the Lord that cost him nothing. David bought the threshing floor and oxen and offered a burnt sacrifice and a communion sacrifice to the Lord. He depended on the mercy of the Lord to end the plague earlier than predicted, and the Lord, appeased by the sacrifices, did so.

Lectio Divina

Spend 8 to 10 minutes in silent contemplation of the following passage:

David's journey through life is similar to the journey of many of us, a journey of sin and repentance, followed by more sin and repentance, and so on. The Lord's patience with David, the repentant sinner, offers hope to all sinners who believe that God will forgive them if they sincerely repent, hoping never to offend the Lord again.

✠ *What can I learn from this passage?*

Review Questions

1. How does the death of Amnon show the ripple effect of sin?
2. Why does David keep forgiving his enemies, as he does with Absalom?
3. Why do the tribes of the northern kingdom (Israel) argue with Judah about who should be the tribes to greet David when he returns as king of all Israel?
4. If David sinned by taking a census, does that mean that our nation sins when it takes a census? Reflect on why God considered this way of David sinful.